Little Runs
Big World

Little Runs Big World

A MARINE'S PATH TO PEACE

Chris Bolender

ISBN: 1516960793
ISBN 13: 9781516960798
Library of Congress Control Number: 2015915037
CreateSpace Independent Publishing Platform
North Charleston, South Carolina

Contents

Thanks, Mom, for convincing me that I'm magic.

A tragedy on run day – 1357 – January 29, 2017

My childhood friend Ryan Owens and I joined the US Navy together and shipped off the summer of 1998. Nearly twenty years later, Ryan was on an operation in Yemen with SEAL Team Six, when he was shot and killed. His soul rests in peace now. He will always be a brother to me.

~RIP Ryan Owens~

Preface

I flew home to Fort Lauderdale from Okinawa, Japan, to attend my best friend's wedding. On the first morning home, I decided to take a jog and loosen up my muscles that were stiff from my cramped twenty-four-hour flight across the Pacific.

I was jogging through Lauderdale-by-the-Sea, a beach town that's a few miles north of the infamous Fort Lauderdale Strip. During the 1980s, the Strip earned a reputation for being a popular party place for college spring-breakers, in large part because of the cheap hotels and easy access to drugs. This hedonistic purlieu was eventually renovated into luxury condos, upscale bars, and shops. Today, the college crowd has faded away, but the Strip remains a major party spot with tamer crowds.

In contrast, Lauderdale-by-the-Sea consists of knickknack tourist shops, seafood restaurants, and a quaint fishing pier. You come to this beach when you want a quiet, romantic place to bring a date—or when you want to have a calm, peaceful jog!

I was here for the latter. My job as a Marine stationed in Okinawa was stressing me out to the point that I no longer felt like myself. Being a commander in charge of 107 Marines and over $100 million of rare national-defense assets was taking its toll on me. I'm pretty sure I didn't smile for an entire month. Ordinarily, I was the life of any party.

I was constantly ordered to take my unit on crucial missions. There was a microscopic margin for error, and failing would result in getting fired. The phrase "Marines never fail" sums up the Marine Corps' hegemony.

I became aggressive, short fused, and confrontational with those who stood in the way of accomplishing the mission. My natural calm and goofy disposition was now dominated by this new edgy persona that the Marine Corps drew out of me by "fracking" my soul with the pressure to succeed. I grew into a bipolar leader who would laugh and banter with those who did great work and chew the asses off those with attitudes or those who were extremely incompetent. Sometimes, I had to confront people I genuinely liked but who were not performing up to my standards. Eventually, all these clashes emotionally drained me, and I became coarse.

I had a constant fear of failing a mission or, worse, a Marine getting hurt. Again, this required more scathing confrontations where I would demand perfection from all those under me.

With the power came great responsibility—and a whole lot of stress. We deployed on new missions every month. I was never home! During this time, if you asked me about my family, I would have said, "I'm not too sure, but I hear they are great people." I missed half my two daughters' birthdays. When I was home, I was usually grumpy or impatient. My hair turned gray, and the angry mask I grew was altering my face with new lines and wrinkles each day.

Even though I was technically on vacation in Florida, I couldn't shake my tension, mainly because I was incredibly nervous over my best-man speech. I wanted it to be a perfect performance. To be on my game, I had to clear out my anxiety, and this was the perfect place to delouse my hectic mind.

I did not plan my running route or set any goals for distance and speed. I just followed my intuition and let go of time. I unleashed my imagination to wander along these streets and this beach. My senses spawned a constant stream of hometown childhood memories. I ran along the tourist shops, weaving in and out of all the window-shoppers.

I was passing my favorite ice cream parlor when the door swung open. A blast of frosty air tapped the right side of my body. I flashed back to holding a sugar cone stacked with two scoops of bubblegum ice cream. I was licking it fast so the hot sun wouldn't melt it. My mom was waiting for me outside with my giant raft and beach toys. She was looking down at me with a smile and didn't say a word; she just watched me enjoy the treat.

I turned away from the stores and followed the scent of breakfast. I knew the smell was coming from my family's favorite restaurant, the Anglins Beach Cafe, where they serve the best breakfast in the world, according to Captain Bolender. This is the only place I've been where the orange juice tastes great served warm and the bacon is always cooked to perfection—crispy but not burnt. The cafe is on the front end of the fishing pier. Half the tables are in a sunroom, and the rest are out on a veranda with an uninterrupted view of the beach and the beautiful Atlantic Ocean.

One guy was petting his small dog and smiling while his partner laughed and sipped his coffee. A brief summer shower surprised the guests. It lasted just long enough to blow a few napkins off the tables and then stopped before it could ruin anybody's Sunday-morning breakfast.

Down the way, a mother rinsed off her toddler's sandy feet while struggling to hold a beach chair and overstuffed beach bag. Plastic rakes and shovels toppled out each time she squatted to brush more sand off him. She told him to do this and that, but he ignored her as he played with his toy boat.

A few senior citizens sat on benches and stared out toward the vast ocean, perhaps replaying their favorite memories while wondering where all the time had gone. A gang of small scavenger birds hopped around them but flew off as I stomped closer.

I ran on the sand and gazed out above the ocean. The morning's amber sunlight shimmered through the dark clouds and projected brightly lit squares on the brown, choppy surf. In South Florida, rain clouds can spring up from nowhere just about any time of the day or night. As kids, we would be playing a game of street football under a sunny sky, and down the street a white squall would be encroaching upon our position. Most of the time, we'd run for cover, sometimes getting caught, other times surrendering. On those really hot summer days, we'd stay put and welcome the cool, drenching rain.

The wind picked up, and the ocean grew agitated. Gusts blew fresh, cool oxygen into my lungs each time I inhaled. The flow of air relaxed me, and I unclenched my fists. I opened up my stride, leaning into the wind—cease, and I'd fall on my face. The wind pressed my cheeks upward. Mother Nature was making me smile as she held me up. I felt the caustic angst flow out of my body. Just like that, my chakras were cleansed. Stress usually evaporates as I run, but this time it was released like a little, black, toxic balloon.

Birds swarmed and dove into the water in a feeding frenzy. Kite surfers farther out were being yanked along the wave tops—it looked fun! I ran by small bunches of people scattered on the sand. One child was stacking moist sand-bucket blocks into a castle while his buddy clawed a moat. A father and son passed a Frisbee. A young teenager skim-surfed on the thin slice of water washing up. The waves rumbled and then fizzed. In between this constant motion of the waves, people chattered and birds cawed.

My hometown runs were filled with scattered, explosive memories that were triggered by familiar smells, sights, and sounds. This beach at Lauderdale-by-the-Sea was a cluttered minefield of memories planted from the time when I was a toddler until I was eighteen. I couldn't take two steps without being whisked away to childhood or my teenage years. Sometimes, one memory would bring on a set of others. Most were precious and gentle, while others would sting just a little.

Memories kept drifting in. My mother brought me here every day until I was five. The crashing sounds of this ocean are part of my consciousness for-ever, similar to how the hollow hum of the sea is trapped inside a conch shell for eternity. Right there in waist-high water is where Meegan Gray knelt on a piece of coral thirty years ago. Blood was everywhere, and we all freaked out. We had to rush her to an emergency room. After the doctor stitched her up, he gave her a green water-tube toy snake that would slip from her grip when she squeezed it. I remembered the details of this toy more than the whole episode. Isn't it crazy how our memories work?

This is where I dropped in on my first wave with my brother Jame's boo-gie board. Another surfing adventure turned treacherous when I swam into the five-foot-long tentacles of a Portuguese man-of-war.

When my friends and I were about fourteen, we'd sneak out of our hous-es and hang out on these sands. The pier provided a nice secluded spot for risqué behavior. Some nights, we'd drink beers with blankets draped over our shoulders while sitting around a blazing campfire. We'd pass around cigarettes as if it were a rite of passage—some refer to this as peer pressure. All these memories made my hometown jogs different from other runs in various parts of the world.

I tuned out the memories and looked forward to tomorrow's wedding night. I started to concentrate on having a good time and living in the moment. I knew that no matter how many times I practiced, I would miss some things. I felt as if that was okay, and I would still enjoy every moment. I no longer worried about it. I was excited to wear my Marine dress uniform and display my medals—always a proud feeling.

I stepped out on the main road, A1A. No cars were in sight. Empty roads give me a sense of empowerment. Cars owned the roads during a weekday rush hour, but in this moment, all the lanes belonged to me. One of those gray clouds ambushed me at about the three-mile mark. In a cynical way, I took joy in watching all the beachgoers panic as if the sky were falling. A lady was slogging against the wind and chasing her beach umbrella as it cartwheeled down the beach. Other people ran with magazines over their heads.

The downpour lasted for a few blocks, and then the rain shut off suddenly, as if someone turned it off from a faucet in the sky. I was drenched on the final homestretch. I sprinted straight down the middle of the slippery road to the next intersection, where I throttled back and began to walk it out toward my car.

From behind me, someone was calling out. "Hey, Marine!"

Did someone actually know that the abbreviation "USMC" on my shirt stands for "United States Marine Corps"? This surprised me because I was hundreds of miles from a military base. Believe it or not, some Americans think that USMC stands for some university or college abbreviation.

The voice came from a lady on a beach cruiser that coasted next to me and then circled around. She hopped off her bike and began to walk with it alongside me. I figured she was married to a Marine and just simply wanted to say hello. This was not unusual; the Marine Corps culture is small, and many of us know each other or at least know someone who knows another Marine.

This particular woman was a friendly looking older lady with a bright smile. She seemed to be the kind of person whom you know you will have a good conversation with. For some reason, I was speechless as she froze and stared deep into my eyes. She seized this moment and could not have cared less if she held up traffic in the middle of the intersection we were standing in.

She stepped a bit closer and whispered. "My son, Sergeant Lea R. Mills, Iraq 2006..." She waited for me to solve her riddle. Then it hit me like a summer squall out of nowhere: her son had died.

I immediately imagined how she got the devastating news. She answers the doorbell to a Marine in his dress uniform with his hat off. A chaplain stands next to him in all black with the exception of his white collar. After they briefly introduce themselves, the Marine tells her that her son was killed in action. She collapses to her knees and screams, burying her head in her trembling hands.

I was frozen as if I suddenly felt all her pain and sensed the presence of Sergeant Mills's spirit. I started to tear up. "IED," she said with a tiny grin. Perhaps she'd grown to finally accept the loss of her son—at least, as much as a mother can.

The amazing aspect of this encounter is that I hadn't said a single word to this stranger up to this point, yet we already shared a connection. I could not fathom her pain. She stepped close and hugged me in a tight squeeze that I've felt several times from my mother when I left and came back from overseas. Thinking about the fact that this woman's son had been a Marine younger than I and that she was a loving mother like mine made me abruptly cry.

We eventually talked, and she told me about how she loves all of us boys (Marines) and she knows her son is still with us. Before I left, she told me her name was Momma Dee, and she gave me a small, square piece of blue nylon with a silver star.

We said our good-byes, and I ran back to my car. Driving away, I steered the car with one hand, while my other hand held the small piece of nylon. I rubbed the fabric between my fingers and thought about how lucky I was to be alive. Feeling the stitches of the embossed star sparked my remaining grief, and tears came out of nowhere and ran down my cheeks. Suddenly, the faucet, like a summer rain, just turned off.

I rolled down the window to let the wind inside, and the breeze cooled my tears. Then, moments later, the tears evaporated as the amber sun shimmered through the trees I passed. I didn't have a worry in the world, because I was happy to be home with my family and friends. I was happy that my mom could still hug me and smile each time I'd come home. I was proud to be a Marine. I was grateful to be alive, and I was ready to be the best man! Bless you, Momma Dee, and rest in peace, Sergeant Lea R. Mills.

This is the type of story you will get in *Little Runs Big World*. This is a memoir tied together by the runs I took while serving in the US military for sixteen years and traveling the world. My runs accompany each triumph and challenge that I encounter on ships, shantytowns, beautiful beaches, and deserts. The run stories are tours of these places and snapshots of the ups and downs throughout my career in the US Navy and US Marine Corps. My life and runs follow paths that fiction could never find and I could never predict.

My story is told from the perspective of a heartbroken eighteen-year-old Navy boy; a twenty-seven-year-old becoming a Marine officer; a terrified thirty-two-year-old committed to a psych ward; a detachment commander in charge of 107 Marines; and a thirty-five-year-old father stationed at Parris Island, South Carolina, transitioning out of the Marines.

These runs took place in Florida, South Carolina, Virginia, Arizona, onboard an aircraft carrier, Dubai, Afghanistan, Egypt Suez Canal, Canada, Japan, Thailand, Vietnam, Guam, and South Korea.

As I ran in these places, I was developing intellectually, emotionally, and spiritually—I was growing up. Before I tell you my stories, you must understand why I run. The chances are that we are all somewhat alike in the way we perceive running. You may not agree with why I run, but you will probably understand the reasons behind why I didn't always enjoy running.

I did not pick up running as a hobby because I was in the military and because that's what military people like doing. On the contrary, we are bred to hate it early on in training, boot camp, and other harsh entry-level schools where running is the main apparatus of discipline and punishment. Marine officers know this all too well. In the Marine Officer "The Basic School," a six-month school for fresh lieutenants, much of the time is spent outside running or hiking.

The Marine Corps specializes in interesting ways to deliver their lesson with pain. My favorite was when they made us do sprints up and down the five-hundred-yard-long rifle range. The fun part was wearing a giant pack filled with about seventy pounds of gear (when dry). Barfing and heat exhaustion were common. Other times, our instructor would stop us in the middle of a run, point to two random guys, and say, "You and you, fight!" Rifles, radios, and all sorts of other gear would fly through the air while we learned how to be warriors, even if that meant broken bones. We learned that most of our "warrior" training occurred on runs, which meant that runs equaled pain.

A large portion of military men and women have become "running haters." The Marine Corps is packed with what some refer to as "twice-a-year runners," or those who run only to complete the mandatory biannual fitness tests. Ask them to join you for a run in between these tests, and they'll laugh at you.

It's not just the military who are bred to hate running. Anyone who's played a sport or participated in gym class may have been turned off from running when he or she was forced to do it. When football players lose games, their coaches punish them with one-hundred-yard sprints, thereby making running a punishment. I would bet that the number of Marines and civilians, per capita, who despise running, is about the same. Who wants to experience forced pain?

The phrase to run has developed a negative connotation because of our collective, myriad bad experiences. We may recall the harsh runs used for punishment and discipline or those stressful dashes we've made to get somewhere in time. Each day that my wife doesn't allot enough time to get ready, she is making a choice to run, scurrying to get to work on time. Whether we are tortured or tardy, we tend to associate running with moments like this.

We hate running to catch a plane. Running for your life when bullies chased you as a kid was horrible! People who actually enjoy that sort of thing must be crazy—runners are nuts. This completely natural act has become negative and a certification for the clinically insane.

I was nine when I first started running, but I can't say that I liked it. My parents ran, so I did. It was apparent how stress-free they were afterward. But I never made the link that running eliminates stress. I never said to myself, "Wow, runs remove stress," or "I think I will run because it makes me feel better." My mom would take me to a local neighborhood track where she would power walk and I'd go for a jog.

Running was painful, and I relied on music to tune out the torture. I'd pop in Bon Jovi's *New Jersey* (1988) cassette tape inside my yellow Sony Walkman, slap the tape door shut, rewind the tape, don my matching yellow headphones, and press the play button. I would then get lost in Bon Jovi's "Bad Medicine" world for three miles. I'm still not sure why I would agree to do this. I hated waking up ridiculously early, and I hated running, but I liked feeling in shape.

My dad also influenced me a bit. He was a random runner. He would just decide on a whim to go for a run. No program or regimen—he just got out and ran. I'll never forget one particular family run when I was twelve years old. On that early, stormy Saturday morning, after finishing our chores, my dad took me, my brother, my sister, and the dog through the neighborhood on a jog.

My dad ignored the hazard of the thunderstorm and led the way through the white squall. I remember trudging through wet grass and stepping into puddles and the cars rushing past us, spraying muddy puddle water all over us. There was no way the drivers could have seen us. I could barely make out what was in front of me. My entire body was drenched, and rainwater streamed down my face. The sky flashed with electric veins, and the clouds crackled and boomed seconds later. This was a bit scary and a little insane.

I remember smiling and feeling a rush of freedom, leaping from puddle to puddle in a storm. Suddenly, nothing mattered because I was in my own little running world. This is the first time I had a glimmer of fun during a run.

After jeopardizing the safety of his entire family, my dad took us out to breakfast to a place called Anglins Beach Cafe on the local Fort Lauderdale fishing pier. All our spirits were high and stress-free. This is when the runner's seed was planted in my subconscious.

I began my career in the Navy at the lowest rank (E-1). My first duty station was on a ship for over three years. I was always homesick. I spent most holidays at sea. I was so miserable at times that I swore off all pleasures, as a monk would do for God, but I was doing it because I was completely dedicated to the times when I'd go home and see my girlfriend. I refused to let go and enjoy myself. I didn't drink soda. I quit going to dance clubs. I cut anything out of my life that made me happy, so I became lonely and depressed.

Having a relationship was extremely difficult. In addition to my life totally sucking, I was insecure and always jealous of other guys who were around my girlfriend. I sweated every weekend, thinking how she was probably cheating on me. On Friday nights, she would be going to a party, and I would be on a ship in the middle of the ocean.

On top of an insecure and miserable existence, my jobs were intense, both physically and mentally. While in the Navy, my job was to defend the ship from missiles and hostile aircraft, which can get a little overwhelming for someone at the age of nineteen. While in the Marine Corps, my job was air defense and military air control—and sometimes this got twice as stressful as any air-traffic-control job in the civilian world. Stress went hand in hand with my military career. The same goes for everyone else in this lifestyle, and everybody has his or her own way to cope.

I realized early on during my Navy career that running was a natural cure for anxiety. "I have yet to have a bad day when I started it with a run," I would often say to myself. I would run here and there, but I was never committed to a system. I just ran whenever and wherever.

Later on, in my thirties, I adopted running into my everyday lifestyle to stay mentally fit. I relied on it to stay sane. Since May 13, 2013, I've run at least one mile per day. The distance is not as important as the consistency. One run plus one run equates to consistency; this is the foundation of a streak. Slow or fast is irrelevant; it is the action that counts. Most of my runs are at a ten-minute-mile pace—the same as my sixty-seven-year-old father. Running is running no matter how slow.

I had been kicking around the idea of streak running, and then one night—while I was heavily intoxicated at a New Year's party, 12:01 a.m. on January 1, 2013—I looked over at my buddy.

"I think I'm going to try and run every day," I said.

"That will never work," he said.

This turned out to be the most motivating thing that anyone has ever told me in my entire life, and it served as the "forever challenge" to my streak running.

I believed that running a mile a day was doable for the rest of my life. This mentality eliminated the burdensome catch-22 of a short-term goal—that is, accomplishing the goal completes the dedicated effort. I wanted to *become* running. I figured that I would always have the ten minutes needed to run a mile and that my body could easily sustain the impact. My first streak lasted ninety-eight days and was broken on the day I was deployed to South Korea with an eight-hour notice. I was too distracted with the planning of a covert mission to run that day.

I got a phone call from my commanding officer. "Hey, Chris. Are you ready to leave in eight hours? We'll need to send you and the usual other five. Come down to the brief that's in thirty minutes."

I was responsible for the success or failure of this mission, and my mind was preoccupied with planning and saturated with the stress that came with it all. That day, I forgot to run. A month or so after the mission was complete, I returned to my home base in Okinawa and began the streak again on May 13, 2013.

I'm telling this memoir through snapshots of my life as I saw it during each run. I will share with you the struggles and glory of being in the military. I will take you on a running tour within cultures all over the world and share with you the unique, beautiful, and crude places. I'll introduce you to the military culture and all its glory and hardship. No extreme running. We'll take a trip along the timeline from my days as a young sailor up until I retired as a much-wiser Marine Corps officer. I invite you to lace up and accompany me on my exciting little runs around this big world.

CHAPTER 1

Running around the World

Onboard an Aircraft Carrier

I n 1998, I went to Navy boot camp at Great Lakes, Illinois, and was transformed from a civilian to a Navy sailor. The process was not easy, and I slowly realized that joining the Navy was a big mistake.

Later, after graduating from boot camp, I shipped out to my school in Pensacola, Florida. The base was on a retired airfield that was once used to teach advanced tactics to World War II and Korean War pilots. The facilities were made out of old hangars. This is where they taught basic principles in electronic warfare and cryptology. School sucked! We had to memorize almost every missile and radar in the world and their capabilities. The school lasted six months and was my first inoculation to the nomadic military lifestyle with its stress and loneliness.

Pensacola became about passing the time. I just wanted to get to the next holiday so I could visit my girlfriend back home. I mostly sat in my room, worked out at the gym, and went for runs on this old airfield, or what was left of it. I would pop my Rage Against the Machine CD into my yellow Sony antiskip disc player—no rewinding necessary!

Nature was erasing the World War II era. I would often hop over some of that war's rusting relics strewn carelessly on the giant airfield. The cayenne pepper was consuming all types of metal-shaped objects, half buried in the weeds or protruding at dangerous angles. A game of night hide-and-go-seek could get you impaled. Patches of grass reached out from the earth to pull apart the crumbling runway. I ran aimlessly to the beat of the music. I had no path and no goal; I was just trying to pass the time.

Most high school graduates would taper away from their golden high school years by going to college and then come home every few months between semesters. Some would stick around, only to be stuck in that routine for the rest of their lives. I took another approach; I ripped the cord right out the wall by shipping off to the Navy.

I was alone for the first time in my life in this new place where nothing was familiar. I was instantly lonely. It was like being dropped into a deserted place in my soul. This new world had its own reality, and I would have to reinvent myself or find myself (I still don't know the difference) in order to survive. This was the beginning of the long and arduous emotional journey of my military career.

I squeaked by to pass the final exam. The electronic-warfare-school instructors placed us in a simulator where we had to operate in a high-stress environment. We had to try to defend our ship from the hundreds of inbound missiles—an impossible feat for any fledging. Because it was insanely difficult, I figured they were merely testing our confidence, so I remained calm and confident and failed proudly. They hammered one principle into us that I would hold on to for life: "If anyone should ask you if you are one hundred percent sure, say yes, because this demonstrates one hundred percent confidence, and confident people are winners."

I got my orders: "Report no later than 0700 on 21 March 1999 to the CVN-75 (Carrier Vessel Nuclear 75), the USS *Harry S. Truman*." My orders placed me on this ship until my end-of-service date on September 8, 2002. This would be my new home for the next three and a half years.

I eventually found myself in the Atlantic Ocean, hundreds of miles off the coast of Africa on this massive, gray, ninety-seven-thousand-ton aircraft carrier the size of three and a half football fields. Fifty-three hundred sailors and Marines were aboard the USS *Harry S. Truman* as it charged eastbound, plunging through the deep swells that were substantial but no challenge for the great vessel. I ran uphill as the bow rose and masked the water below.

Moments later, I'd find myself in a relaxed stride downhill as the bow lowered to reveal a beautiful, deep-blue ocean.

It felt as if I were out jogging on the Jolly Green Giant's enormous seesaw. The *Truman* was the largest floating air base in the world and longer than the Empire State Building is tall. As the days wore on, my runs on the ship became more and more comfortable. It's funny how humans can eventually get used to practically anything. I would twist and crane my neck to see over the edge of the ship. Ninety feet down, the steel hull gobbled up the sea and created monster hydraulics that were big enough to swallow an entire team of kayakers.

The swirling, slapping, and churning produced fresh, white foam that would follow us for only a few moments before it fizzled out. "Keep 'em steady!" I told myself after my knees turned to jelly from the thought of falling into the white whirlpools. There was a popular sea story going around that this one sailor jumped overboard and drowned in ice-cold Halifax, Canada. Navy divers eventually found his body. Autopsies revealed that he had been stuck under the keel for weeks. When they hoisted his waterlogged, pale corpse to the surface, it was withered like baitfish that had been trolled for hours or, in his case, after a two-thousand-mile trip back to Norfolk, Virginia.

My first run was a welcomed respite from the weeks of artificial lighting and breathing the stuffy, recycled air in the decks below for over a month. Up on deck was amazing. I pulled the sea breeze in through my nose. I almost felt as if I were on a normal beach with piercing bird calls overhead and the sound of crashing waves.

Seven or eight seabirds glided into the wind in a tight V formation, with one side longer than the other. Maybe they'd been cooped up too. But where had they come from, and why were they so relaxed, so free? Maybe there were some deserted islands nearby. Maybe they stowed themselves away inside one of the ship's open bays before we left our home port in Norfolk. Were they lost? Or maybe we picked them up when we barreled through a big storm. Did they know how far they were from their own skies? Did they care? This ship was a city that held over eighty aircraft and over five thousand people, so I figured there was plenty of room for a few lost birds. They would be captured if spotted near an aircraft, but no animal on earth would want to draw close to this flight deck, which sounded like a war zone during flight operations.

Planes land on an aircraft carrier by slamming down hard enough for their tailhook to catch the arresting wire. Loud thumps. They land with their afterburners on full blast so they can keep flying if they miss their trap: sounding like a thunderous blowtorch. Then the loudest, the booms from the catapults—the mechanism in the tracks of the flight deck. It slings jets and prop planes off the runway from 0 to 165 miles per hour in two seconds—faster than any drag-race car. The piece called a tow bar is fixed to the bottom of the jets. The BOOM is made when the tow bar hits the end of the track and releases the plane.

I was on the ship, sleeping in my coffin rack (bunk) the first time I ever heard the deftly loud boom. The unannounced explosion jolted me out of my bunk. I rolled out to investigate and ran through the narrow passageway toward the sound. A sailor caught on and set this rookie straight.

"They're just testing the catapults, bro," he said, grinning.

The birds' V formation canted and banked around the side of the gray, eight-story tower. The superstructure had a white "75" stenciled on the side in house-sized font—its number designator. A line of streamers flapped in the wind. The radars and sensors brought all eight levels to life with gray bubbles, spinning bars, spinning dishes, and gray octagons. All sorts of poles and antennas sprouted out the sides. Surprisingly, the minuscule spinning radar was the most important device for navigation, and all the others were necessary to accomplish our objectives—they were our eyes and ears.

Ah, fresh air and sunshine! I leaned into the stiff head wind and kept running onward, almost jogging in place. Sometimes, we would be coasting along at a pretty good pace. The huge hunk of steel could get up and go in a hurry when it needed to. Aircraft carriers are actually the fastest ships in the fleet. Their high-speed capability helps them evade an enemy and is necessary to launch aircraft. Something was surreal about the 360-degree blue view I had while running on something so incredibly large that floated.

The ship and the experiences were amazing, but I didn't appreciate her grandeur because I was stuck in the quicksand of homesickness. My mind was constantly occupied with thoughts of my high school sweetheart. I couldn't pull the ripcord and let her go. We had been in a long-distance relationship for two years, but we never experienced the gauntlet of a deployment overseas for 180 days. How I longed for our relationship to be as sturdy as the ship I was on—a vessel that could endure a hurricane without deviating one degree.

I hated the amount of time that I would be gone, so I wished it away. It made me sick! I made a massive countdown of the time I had remaining in the Navy. I had 1,743 meals, 581 days, 2 baseball seasons, and 1 football season left in my enlistment. I also quantified what I had left in the 180-day deployment. I was desperate and did more than count down. I would obsess to find tangible evidence that we were moving through time—some version of time rings, like those you would find on a tree stump. I accounted for the wear and tear on the flight deck and the black skid marks from jet tires super-imposed on the fading white-and-yellow runway lines.

When I first boarded the ship, she looked like a toy model, freshly paint-ed with bright, white, shiny stickers. Now there was wear and tear. Time had passed. There was proof. I also realized that I could fast-forward the journey by sleeping twelve hours a night. This meant that I would be conscious for only half the days remaining. With little sunlight on my skin and ample sleep, I don't think I aged a bit during this deployment. The face-numbing cold berthing produced a cryogenic effect.

All these techniques just seemed to generate more angst. The older and wiser men suggested that I break up with my girlfriend so I could just let go and enjoy myself. Most relationships, even marriages, fall victim to the deployment gauntlet. There are all types of sea stories about men coming home to find oth-er men literally sleeping in their beds. I heard unsettling tales of wives divorcing their husbands and cleaning out all their money while the husbands were at sea. Or faithful wives would find out their husbands solicited sex in a third-world country. Infidelity is the common relationship killer. The old-timers sug-gested that I become single so I could seek out tours and other fun activities at each port we visited. I accepted most of their life advice; however, on this topic, I would not listen. In my heart, I was certain that this girl was the one.

I spent a large part of my free time on pay phones getting all worked up because she didn't answer the phone. At sea, a phone call cost a dollar per minute. I burned through stacks of phone cards and stacks of cash. I completely lost control one day when I found out that she had been lying to me about going to the library on the weekends. A week later, I found out that the "library" was a college dance club near Florida State University. I couldn't do anything about it except kick some sand and throw a few pity parties. It wasn't just her. I did my fair share of chasing skirts. Long distance sucked!

A couple of weeks later, I was topside again. The gray deck was smoldered with more black soot marks from about a month's worth of afterburner exhaust. The water was still as we idled through the Suez Canal. The crashing white water was now mere bathtub splashes. All operations were on pause, and chaos took a break to catch its breath.

We were puttering through the Suez Canal, an area known to some as "The Ditch." The artificial waterway in Egypt extends from Port Said to Suez and connects the Mediterranean Sea with the Red Sea. The Ditch is a tight squeeze, sort of like inching your way along a crowded movie-theater aisle. I could throw a Frisbee onto land. Peering cautiously over the edge, I could see bright-green grass ninety feet straight down. This time, I had a little more confidence about getting close to the edge because I finally had my so-called sea legs, a skill that can be achieved only after weeks of rocking in the ocean. Sailors on the smaller ships, called "small boys," develop extraordinary sea legs and can continue to walk on the walls when the ship rolls from side to side.

Trolling through this canal at this particular time made me a bit paranoid. It had been only three months since Al Qaeda's attack on a Navy ship, the USS *Cole* (DDG-67), just fifteen hundred miles south of where we were. The following is from an FBI report:

> On October 12, 2000, suicide terrorists exploded a small boat alongside the USS *Cole*—a Navy destroyer—as it was refueling in the Yemeni port of Aden. The blast ripped a forty-foot-wide hole near the waterline of the *Cole*, killing seventeen American sailors and injuring many more.

For those in the US Navy, this had a similar impact that September 11, 2001, would later have on the rest of America.

Snipers scanned for possible threats. Helicopters chopped overhead with machine guns sticking out the sides like oars. The nearby villages were all ghost towns. Why were they abandoned? Maybe there had been farms and a hustling-bustling town. Bright-green grass was along the waterside, and a bridge was arching over the deserted background. The bridge hadn't yet been fused together. Construction crews on both sides of the bridge sparked and clanked as they worked to join up and finish the five-hundred-foot structure.

My friends and I started a rumor on board that the bridge would be finished soon and would delay our trip home because we would have to sail around the Horn of Africa. Ship rumors spread like a virus, so we'd make them up for entertainment's sake. Rumors that dealt with going home early or staying out longer always caught on quickly because everyone was desperate to get home and see their loved ones. The most famous rumor from an unknown source was that we would have to pull into a port for three months to have our flight deck resurfaced. I still chuckle to myself at times about this one.

Our mission in the Persian Gulf was to act as the main effort in Operation Southern Watch. Our aircraft flew combat air patrols that policed the no-fly zone. A month after George W. Bush took office, he authorized a deadly strike package on Iraq to take out their command-and-control radar and communication sites. No one knew what to expect, and everyone was nervous. We saw over twenty aircraft take off with bombs loaded. They left *wings dirty* and came back *wings clean*. As the pilots take off, it is naval tradition for the flight crew to align on the side of the runway and salute as the pilots fly into a combat situation. They all returned safe on deck, and that was the last we heard about our mission.

In our electronic-warfare room, we had an infrared, closed-circuit television that showed only the flight deck. On late nights, this made for good entertainment, as we watched aircraft miss their landings. They would come down hard and fast, and their tailhooks would fling sparks in all directions. Their afterburners glowed white hot, and when they missed their trap, they would flare as the aircraft furiously pulled up and flew away.

Our next port call was canceled. We were scheduled to visit Dubai, United Arab Emirates, the following day, but our commanding officer was uneasy about a possible Iraqi retaliation. "In place of our port call, we will hold a Steel Beach Picnic," the commanding officer said over the ship's intercom.

A Steel Beach Picnic is what it sounds like: a picnic on a steel beach or, in this case, a ship. However you brand it, it's a lame party on the flight deck. It's as if you tell a kid he can have cottage cheese after you've promised him chocolate ice cream. As lame as such picnics were, I enjoyed the sunlight and cool breezes. Anytime I could surface, I felt better. Some of the sailors threw together a band and jammed out some popular rock music.

A loud airplane in the distance headed our way. When it flew over us at about five hundred feet, it looked much like an airliner. I later found out that it was an Iranian P-3 military jet and that Iran did this sort of thing all the time. This plane was not equipped with weapons, so it wasn't a serious threat. They were just marking their territory. This kind of thing reminded me that we were not in friendly waters.

Weeks after our Steel Beach Picnic, we finally made it into Dubai. The first thing I saw when I disembarked the ship were fence banners around the construction sites with the text, "Bin Laden Construction." Um...Bin Laden? Where the hell were we? Of course, this was not *the* Bin Laden, the notorious terrorist, but his wealthy family. It happens that he was wealthy in his preterrorist days.

I passed up the wise advice from elder sailors to have fun and instead went right to the pay-phone bank. I couldn't get ahold of my girlfriend. I called. I called. I struggled. Finally, I ran.

I wasn't free to run in Dubai; actually, no one was free to roam the streets. We all walked right off the ship into a sort of holding-prison compound nicknamed by service members as "The Sandbox." Inside the compound was a series of game and food booths along with a concert stage in the center. I ran along the fence line by a series of towers where snipers glassed for threats beyond our fortified perimeter.

This was nothing more than a prison with a county fair in the middle. Vendors sold food and showcased clothes for sale that dangled in the dusty breeze. The light-brown haze from the powdery Arabian sand coated everything. Who the heck would buy a dingy, brown-white shirt? Lots of guys bought them because they said "Dubai" on them. You could buy any fake brand-named clothing and accessories, including "Foakleys" (fake Oakley sunglasses), imposter Louis Vuitton purses, and cologne that smelled the way I recalled cologne smelling. These venders licked their chops at the sight of sailors with bloated pockets who had been out to sea for a month with nothing to spend their money on.

Everyone was dressed in civilian clothes, pretending to be out on the town and having a great time. I ran past a couple of car salesmen with their claws slowly gripping the backs of their prey and showing off the leather interior of some cars the sailors could not afford and didn't need. These sharks were selling cars out of magazines in the middle of the desert! Who the hell wants to buy a car when he or she is on a quest at sea?

The sun was setting to live music onstage. I circumvented the crowd, which was catching up on thirty alcohol-free days at sea. Most were already wasted, and some were sandwiched in between skimpily clad dancers, writhing to the sounds of the techno music. Did these provocative drunk dances lead to sex? Did married men and women do this kind of thing? Yes and yes.

We would eventually visit Dubai again, and were able to leave the Sandbox. One of my friends went on a guided tour where he raced through the desert dunes at 110 miles per hour in a Land Rover. After this exhilarating jaunt, he visited a small village where he drank tea and ate native food with a talon on his shoulder. I spent a few days of liberty obsessing over the phones, but I did make it out for a day of fun at the Wild Wadi Water Park in Dubai. This park had an uphill slide! The people here were dressed strangely. Some wore turbans. Some women wore *abayas* at the park; whereas, others wore swimsuits like you'd see at any other water park. Children splashed, played, yelled, and laughed as they'd run through the splash pads. The kids there played like kids do everywhere. In that moment, I wished that kids all over the world could play without ever worrying about war again.

CHAPTER 2

Torture: A Flashback to My Tough Beginning

My harshest training in the Marines lay in the shadows of my youth-football torture. These early days defined me. They gave me the strength to push through future challenges. They made me hate running!

Summer football practices in South Florida are no joke. They either kill you or make you into a tougher football player. A typical day between July and August averages around ninety degrees Fahrenheit and 91 percent humidity. It gets even hotter when you're wearing helmets; shoulder pads; and the uniform made of long, polyester, padded pants and jerseys (with the little holes). Lucifer would quit.

After practice, my wadded-up, sweat-drenched jersey would splat when I threw it on the tile floor of the laundry room. Every item had to be hung on the fence to dry or washed each day after practice. During my days on the Northeast Rebels, a peewee-league football team, from the age of eight to fourteen, heat and humidity provided the natural foundation of our misery. Coaches used these unforgiving conditions as a foundation for their program of pain. These men were the most dangerous element, and they could have killed any one of us. If one of us baked to death, they would be indicted shortly after the prosecutor found overwhelming evidence that the coaches prevented their players from drinking water.

Our coaches saw water as a privilege, not a right. What were they thinking? It doesn't take some official study to prove that dehydration kills and that a child dehydrates faster than an adult. The coaches wanted to win, and we thirsted for water. The water prohibition was bullshit; Marine boot camp and Officer Candidates School won't even play this game! A drill instructor could go to prison.

Another torture tool, besides denying our water rights, was running. Running was the coaches' version of waterboarding. It was delivered in two ways: the first was to punish and discipline the team for poor performances, and the second was used for rapid weight loss.

The Northeast Rebels City League football had three levels: big team, middle team, and small team. Each level had a separate weight class, and there was zero leeway on the game-day weigh-ins. To meet the requirement, all players needed to weigh at or below the specific weight and not a pebble over. When I was eighty-nine pounds, four pounds above the limit, I had to run. My insane coaches made us "fat kids" run with garbage bags underneath sweat suits. Coaches welcomed steamy-hot days to reduce water weight faster. Cut a hole for the head and arms, and voila!

On the death runs, I would feel water constantly beading from my shoulders into my cotton jogging pants. I realize now that any of these runs could have easily killed me. I would run for about an hour with my headphones on. The music and my motivation for the upcoming game kept me going. I was our center lineman, an essential position. My team relied on me. I would find some black asphalt to get my jogging suit nice and toasty so that I could roast faster. I remember running back to the so-called weigh-in headquarters, which was in the small, concrete building that housed the restrooms, concession stand, and scale.

Outside my tunnel vision was a whitewashed background with purple dots. Nobody was in sight. I could have passed out from heatstroke and died a couple hundred feet away. They would have found my "fat," eighty-nine-pound, pale body rotting in the hot sun.

One time, I was still overweight after running for hours. I stripped down to my soaking-wet, white underwear and stepped on the old-fashioned balance scale. The metal tab hit the top of the square and clanked. I was still a couple of pounds over. The obese equipment coach studied the scale to see if it would suddenly change. It stayed pinned to the top. He spit a mouthful of tobacco on the sidewalk.

"You only got two pounds left, little bugger!" he said. "Now go on and get them keys from coach. You still got a couple hours." Dying for thirst and foaming at the mouth, I proceeded to the next step where they turned the heat up a notch—literally.

The ignorance! The key to coach's rusty, puke-green El Camino had a fuzzy, dingy-white lucky rabbit's foot attached. His car backfired and stalled at intersections, but that heater worked great. I pushed the lever all the way to the right on the highest heat setting. The sun baked those hot, tan leather seats, and my mouth was dry, as if I'd eaten a pile of sawdust. The steady stream of hot air whistled out and sizzled my eyebrows. The sensation put me to sleep each time. I woke up to the smell of brine from my baking skin. I stepped out, and an amount of sweat that could've filled a 7-Eleven Big Gulp spilled to the ground. For some reason, I remember running being worse than coach's car.

The coach nodded. "Good job, Bolender. You're eighty-three pounds. You can play today. You already weighed in, so you can go get something to drink."

If this hadn't worked, I would have been told to throw up—I had to resort to this only once. After I made weight, it was time to take a few steps to stay alive. After game-day weigh-ins, a designated team mom would wait around the corner with a cooler packed with ice-cold Gatorades, bananas, and whatever else you give a severely dehydrated nine-year-old boy with malnutrition. She tended to all the "fatties." I wonder if she was part of the Red Cross chapter for abused children or just a stupid, naïve, bad mother.

Thanks for the Gatorade, but why the hell didn't you call the police? These humanitarian moms rotated out each game day. I look back now and realize how ridiculous this was. No one actually asked the existential question, "Why are these kids risking their lives?" or "Why are we dumb enough to enable it?"

I wonder if the team coordinator ever sent home a letter with the kids to solicit their mothers to help enable this nonsense. They should have sent a letter to the paramedics instead—at least they would've been more effective in reviving the dehydrated youths, and they would've ensured that no one died of heat stroke. I imagine the letter would go something like this:

Dear Parents,

Please show your support by volunteering one of ten game-day Saturdays this season to replenish our abused, overheated, and dehydrated fat children on our team. If we help them recover from the self-inflicted heat exhaustion, they may not die. Remember that they are sealed in black body bags—I mean, garbage bags (he-he)—and forced to run until their asses melt off. The ones who don't make weight after these perilous runs may have to sit in coach's shitty car with the heat on full blast. Even more extreme are the ones who have to vomit their essential fluids out as if their stomachs are being pumped for an overdose.

Note: Bananas help quell the damage. Not an ounce of water is given to the boys for hours, so have plenty of water for our Tigers. Remember, parents, that a life may depend on your participation. They can literally die if you don't, and we don't want to be indicted on manslaughter. Let's risk their lives for a winning season! Go-o-o-o Tigers!

Chow,

Mrs. Roboyta (Team Mom)

P.S.: Remember, those bananas restore potassium in their little, starved, severely dehydrated bodies.

I hated the runs and almost died in that crappy El Camino, but I enjoyed winning games. And parents approved, so it had to be right. There was even a harsher type of running than the body-bag miles. "Suicides" were one-hundred-yard sprints in quick succession with little time in between for breathing.

After embarrassing losses or too many penalties, my coaches chose to use this painful drill, much as an evil doctor would choose his favorite stainless-steel torture tool from a variety of others tucked in a fabric, rolled case.

The "Great Mass Suicide Session of 1990" occurred one Monday night after our second-straight loss, 21 to 0 against the Spartans. They were notoriously the worst team every year. Coach was embarrassed, and we would pay. After the game, he huddled us up. He paced back and forth for a long, silent minute. He would pause to look at one of us, and right before cussing him out, he'd pace again, stop again and stare, and pace again, and on and on. He finally cooled down enough to speak. He said the absolute worst thing to us.

"Come to practice Monday in full pads." Then he walked away.

He should have told us to make our wills before Monday.

Mondays were usually a recovery day. We'd dress in shorts, T-shirts, and helmets—no pads. This Monday was a full-on practice that went into overtime. Around 8:30 p.m., after "normal" practice ended, we were held hostage on a dark field, well after the stadium lights were turned off. We stood thirty abreast across the width of the field as if we were facing a firing squad. Coach was armed with the most dangerous weapon that a pissed-off coach could possess: the silver whistle.

He delivered the blows in short bursts. *TWEET!* We sprinted to the other goal line and back, one hundred yards each way. Our helmets and shoulder pads got heavier with each dash. The pitch of his whistle grew higher each time he blew it. No mercy. We sprinted a stupid number of times, and most of us puked out the pink pickled eggs and raspberry ICEEs we had bought from the concession stand and scoffed down minutes before practice. *TWEET! TWEET! TWEE-E-E*—We didn't stop until our stomachs were emptied out and half the team was crawling.

A line of amber-colored, dimmed lights—parents idling in the parking lot with their dimmers on—snaked around the field. Parents thought this was fine, so it had to be all right. Can we blame their ignorance? It was the

'80s, and people still questioned the fact that smoking kills. It was such a naïve era.

I hate to admit it, but the torture worked. We never lost another game the rest of the season. We all risked our lives. I guess the coach believed that risking jail time was a small price to pay for an 8-and-2 season. I survived. The team survived. Peewee football became my well of fortitude that I tapped into during my brutal Marine-officer training thirteen years later. Deep in this well is where I would find my strength. I definitely hated running, but I knew I would never need to stop no matter how hot it got and no matter how close I was to dying.

CHAPTER 3

Climbing Mount Trashmore (and Down Again)

Mount Trashmore, Virginia Beach, was a reclaimed garbage dump that was refurbished in the 1970s into biohazard-free playgrounds, fishing ponds, and a skate park without swarms of vultures. It was covered in grass and somehow didn't stink. I trained running on this heap for two years and increased my speed tremendously to make myself a more competitive college football player.

It was a little past first light on a Saturday morning, and the sun was already scalding. No breeze was present to evaporate the humidity off my clammy forehead. It was already a hot day. My superior officer's seventeen-year-old son and I took a breather at the top of the hill to watch the traffic on Highway 64 buzz through the stagnant, patchy smog. The park would come to life in a bit. For now, though, just a couple of early-riser yardbirds were moving around down there. Some walked their dogs.

I was coaching the boy. "Choppy steps. Come on, pump your arms! On your toes. That's it!" I had received the day off in exchange for providing some pro-bono speed training. I had perfected my own training techniques over the past two years, and in about six months, I'd be trying out for the Florida Atlantic University football team. My efforts on this hill made me into college material. I didn't mind passing the flame on to someone who could hack it, someone who wanted it badly enough.

The boy claimed to be in shape, so I didn't bother with holding back. Our parlay consisted of uphill sprints, downhill slaloms through an obstacle of tiny orange cones, fifty-meter dashes with a parachute attached to our waists, uphill backward shuffles with a weighted vest, and one-hundred-meter suicide sprints on flat ground—the kind my peewee coach had loved to torture us with.

The boy lasted for an hour and then bent over and propped his hands up on his knees, gasping for air. He took a knee and tried to throw up but dry heaved instead. He was paying the price to the hill gods to become better. We called it a day, and I never saw him again. He didn't have what it takes. He became another victim of torture by running. He probably never ran again, and the poor guy would never look at a parachute the same way—ever.

I felt the same pain and paid the hill gods as he had done, but the difference was that I had what it takes. He was still in high school, unlettered, and living out his last phase of innocence. I had been doing hard time in the Navy, and my eagerness to play the sport I loved was insatiable. My abysmal lifestyle while being stuck on a ship for almost four years served me well because I had no distractions to sidetrack me from accomplishing my dream. I felt I was wasting time in the Navy, but if I used the *wasted time* to get to my dream, then I would be vindicated. My hopes for playing football started on the first day I went aboard the ship where I would live for almost four years.

I reported to the USS *Harry S. Truman* as an E-1, the lowest enlisted rank in the Navy.[1] Another junior Sailor gave me a warm welcome. He greeted me on the quarterdeck, grabbed one of my three bags, and smiled. "I'm so glad that you're here! As a matter of fact, I've been looking forward to your check-in since we got the word. Come on, I'll show you around the ship and bring you to where you'll be working for the next year."

I was immediately lost. An aircraft carrier has more than ten levels, and every fifty feet are posted maps on the wall that read, "YOU ARE HERE." The maps looked like the schematics of a circuit board to me—they never helped a damn.

Getting lost for about three months is the only way to gain your bearings. The suspense built up. We went through hatches, climbed up dozens

---

1 Military enlisted ranks are E-1 through E-9. Officer ranks are O-1 through O-9.

of ladders, and passed through several passageways, scooting by hundreds of other Sailors in the process. Surely he was taking me to some top-secret space or some underground, illegal counterfeit-purse store, akin to the hidden stores in big cities like Seoul or New York.

Unfortunately, he didn't take me to some high-tech, electronic-warfare room with fancy screens, blue lights, and high-ranking officials making life-and-death decisions. We walked down below, and he opened the unmarked door to the head (restroom). Then he handed me a swab (mop). "It's pretty self-explanatory. Just remember to come find me if you see brown water come up from the drains. These heads back up about once a week."

For a year, I never did my job. I was convinced that all electronic-warfare training was a joke. I did various jobs, but defending the ship from missiles was not one of them. I swept, swabbed, and waxed decks; painted chipped paint; scrubbed stalls, toilets, and showers; dewatered the head when the sewage water backed up once a week; sorted the trash at the chow hall[2]; washed dishes; humped mail and food to and from the decks above and below; and stood four-hour Dumpster guard watches.

Even the ship's visitors treated me like a peasant when I did mess duty. One time a VIP, a famous Fox News reporter, didn't even say thanks when I served her drinks and took away her soiled plate; this fifteen-year grudge just recently expired. Dumpster watch was even more absurd than ungrateful VIPs. The Dumpster guard would stand his post to ensure trash was sorted accordingly and abide by the Navy's second general order: "To walk my post in a military manner, keeping always on the alert, and observing everything that takes place within sight or hearing."

It was imperative to keep always on alert to ensure cardboard did not mix with paper.

This was boring and extremely painful on windy winter nights. The line of trash containers was located on a pier in between two aircraft carriers, so

2 Garbage was sorted into discarded food, shells and bones, plastics, and paper. Plastics were melted into giant hockey-puck-shaped disks. Paper was burned. The shells and bones were put into burlap sacks and tossed overboard. Sorting this was disgusting!

the space between the behemoths would cause a wind tunnel. The wind off the Chesapeake River would whistle through the tunnel, and her icy breath blew deep into the marrow of my cheekbones and chiseled at my sinuses.

The first year was the worst time of my Navy experience. I felt duped by the propaganda, the commercials, and the recruiters. They didn't show this crap on their commercials. A more realistic advertisement would say the following:

> Come join the US Navy, and you can see the world while living on a ship! Guard Dumpsters from evil cardboard. Sign up now and we guarantee that, in a few months, you'll be sorting through slimy garbage and pumping the finest, sweet-smelling sewage out of restrooms that we call heads!

I'll never forget what one recruit at boot camp said to me while I scrubbed tile grout with a toothbrush and he dusted the floor nearby with socks over his hands to wipe up the dust bunnies. He paused from his work and looked me right in the eye. "Pssst, hey, you wanna know what the Navy stands for? It's an acronym." He looked around as if he were about to disclose top-secret information. "Never Again Volunteer Yourself!"

I felt as if I had ruined my life by joining the Navy and putting myself on this prison-like ship. In my time, Sailors shared eerie similarities with prisoners. Neither were free to come and go as they pleased. Both wore blue dungarees and black boots—although Sailors had to wear black socks that stained their feet; whereas, prisoners enjoyed white cotton. We both slept on bunks with the same blue-and-white-striped mattresses and pillows.

I was served a "sentence" that was longer than what some do for murder. I faced the truth that joining had been a bad choice. I bought a few *Chicken Soup for the Soul* books and cried to my mom dozens of times until I discovered a possible solution. I would use this incarceration period to build a bridge to something greater. I decided to train to become a college football player.

My first step was to gain weight. As in a prison, we had tons of gym access. I began a strict weight-lifting program. I was 185 pounds and needed to get to 230 pounds and build some major strength. I invested a large portion of the few dollars they paid me[3] into the whole suite of "get big" supplements. Amino acids, protein, and creatine were my new staples. I ingested them in many ways. I had the stuff you shake, the stuff that fizzles, and the pills you take.

Within a year, I bulked up from 190 to 210 pounds and was getting stronger. A fellow Sailor, a mountain man from the Smoky Mountains, sized me up. "Dang, son. Them shoulders look like footballs!"

I could bench-press 305 pounds and lift 225 pounds over my head from a sitting military press.

I was still lacking in the other major benchmark: speed. The crucial forty-yard dash was a major metric for college football. For encouragement, I would tell myself that I better sprint forty yards in five seconds or stay home because I wouldn't be able to play for any team.

During the summer of 2000, my buddy clocked my speed for the first time: 7.2 seconds. That's fast for a three-legged race but disgusting for an aspiring college football player. Oh boy, I was in big trouble.

My first call[4] for advice was to an expert in the field—namely, my brother Big J, who had been a college football player for Jackson State (Mississippi) in 1992. He had weighed 330 pounds and sprinted forty yards in 4.8 seconds—lightning fast for a lineman. This speed was unheard of for a man his size, and he attributed his unique ability to the tough training regimen he'd performed for years. His advice was to run the steepest hill over and over until I barfed.

---

3 For the first six months in the Navy, I made less than $200 a week. The Navy justified our sparse pay by saying that we get three hots (meals) and a cot. I would argue that a prisoner could earn as much making license plates while receiving most of the same benefits.

4 The Internet wasn't mainstreamed yet, and Google was a start-up company less than two years old that very few people had heard of in 2000. Books and people were the main source of information for most before the year 2000.

He made hills sound like gods that would bestow speed upon me if I offered a sacrifice in the form of sweat and tears. I needed to pay the hill gods.

The nearest hill to my base in Norfolk, Virginia, was Mount Trashmore. It was a coincidence that I would begin my training on an old dump site while holding a forty-yard time that was itself trash. This was the biggest hill in town, and I was going to run up and down it until my forty-yard time dropped. I had a simple workout plan: I would sprint up the hill until my legs gave out. I had no natural strength in my legs, and the more I trained, the worse I felt. Damn, I was slow. But I stayed on this old dump until I didn't stink.

For months, I paid the hill gods gallons of sweat and buckets of tears. I had a friend clock me again. I was worse than when I started. I ran a 7.5. What was going on? I found the nearest pay phone and made a collect call to Big J. I was at a 7-Eleven pay phone and wearing compression shorts and cleats.

I cried to him. "How did I become worse? I stink even more!"

He asked me to explain my entire regimen for the past few months. Like an old and wise Japanese sensei, he had wisdom that was very short and concise. "You must run downhill, too, dummy!" He chuckled, and my cry transitioned into a hybrid cry-laugh. I was a snotty mess, but I had the magic key.

Apparently, running downhill is just as important in speed training as going up. Running uphill gives you strength, but downhill trains your brain and hip flexors to relax to allow your legs to cycle faster. In a few weeks, I improved to a 6.5. I had six months left until my active service ended, and I was 225 pounds with a decent forty-yard time down to a 5.8. I was on track toward 5.0. My goals were manifesting into reality.

The news story about a Sailor getting out to play college football was good media for the Navy, so the ship's press featured mine on the front page of their newspaper and made me into a ship celebrity. This got awkward. One morning, while eating breakfast, the guy seated across from me held the newspaper in front of his face while he slurped his cereal. I was on the cover. He lowered the paper to glare at me and then stopped chewing for a second. After he confirmed that I was the guy, he raised the paper again, and I was left to stare at myself during breakfast.

The article had been written on our way to my hometown, Fort Lauderdale, Florida. All operations ceased during this time, so I was freshly oxygenated, and the entire crew was well rested and ready for liberty. Most were in jovial moods; the jokes and laughter abounded throughout the decks.

I woke up at first light and went for the most pleasant run I had ever taken on the flight deck. This run was more stable than the run in the Suez Canal. This time, the land looked familiar. We were anchored a mile off Port Everglades, Fort Lauderdale, just outside the range of a pelican but far enough away where buildings turned to mushy lights. I sucked in the cool fog and reminisced about my entire Navy career—just me, the bronze Atlantic, and the lighted coastline of my home.

Fort Lauderdale was once thousands of different people whom I didn't know. But on this morning, they all whispered in the same voice to me. They were all one organism: my hometown. My two worlds were colliding. I was bringing the Navy home. I had only a couple of months left in the Navy, and I was lucky enough to be riding my ship into my hometown port. I had so much to look forward to. I would soon show my parents and everyone I grew up with what I'd been up to for the past four years. I was stoked. I sat on the edge of the ship and listened to the soft claps of the water on her hull. The ninety-foot drop didn't scare me this time. If I fell off the ship now, I could probably swim home from here.

That afternoon, five hundred Sailors wore their white uniforms and manned the rails[5] on the flight deck around the perimeter of the ship. I stood with them on the edge in my Dixie cup.[6] A blimp drifted overhead and scrolled a "Welcome Home" message. News helicopters swarmed. This was a surreal part of my dream come true that I had not planned on—a bonus. Apparently, this bonus made for a good news story in Fort Lauderdale because the local Channel 10 reporter interviewed me. His story was all about a Sailor following his dream of playing college football. The story seemed

---

5 Manning the rails is a naval tradition that occurs when a ship pulls into a port. Sailors face outboard, lining the perimeter in their dress white uniforms with their hands behind their backs.

6 A Dixie cup is the white, bowl-shaped/Dixie cup-shaped hat that sailors wear.

to catch on, because I was attending the local university, Florida Atlantic University (FAU). The reporter ended his five-minute local segment with a cheesy line: "Bolender is trading his radar screen for a screen pass."[7]

The Navy let me out a few months early so I could try out for the FAU football team. When I got home, I had a few weeks before tryouts, so I called upon a local-county track coach—one of the best in the state. I paid him with a massage roller I still had in the box (an old gift). He taught me some techniques that I still utilize today.

"Hold your tongue to the roof of your mouth, and breathe in through your nose," he said.

His training was all about building up stamina. We ran along Fort Lauderdale Beach in knee-high water. He taught me a few other tips on how to stretch and relax. He was the first person who gave me one-on-one training since my beginning on Mount Trashmore. He validated my training program and also clocked me a few times before sending me on my way.

"You did all the hard work already. Now go show those twerps what you're made of," he said with strong encouragement.

I woke up with the same excitement I'd had on the brisk Christmas morning of 1987 when I finally got a black ninja suit. I had asked Santa for it the year before, but my parents couldn't afford it, so they told me that a poor kid in Argentina got the only one left.

Anticipation boiled over. Now was the time for the most important run of my life. I awoke and did what I'd promised myself years before: I watched the film *Varsity Blues*. Then I cried and laced up.

I showed up with a T-shirt that said "Navy" on the back. I wanted these coaches to know that I was a seasoned man, much saltier than these teenagers. They would soon see that I had what it takes. About forty candidates showed up. There was no way these guys were as serious and as ready as I was.

---

7 Before my wife and I started dating, she saw this news report and told her friend, "I want a man like Chris Bolender." We ended up married with two kids. I joke with her that she had been stalking me since the day I was fresh off the boat.

The first challenge was to run the forty yards three times. I stuck at 5.2 on each one—all that work for a few sprints. The next challenge was to run as far as I could in twelve minutes. The coach yelled out loud and clear, "On your marks. Get set. Go!"

I shot off like an F-14 from the *Truman* and quickly dug deep into my well of fortitude to make each stride count. All the training from Mount Trashmore, all the crap I had cleaned on board the ship, and all the hard labor I had done to get here flashed before me. I nailed the run again with two miles in twelve minutes. Only one other guy was faster than I, and he was trying out for wide receiver, one of the faster positions in football. Apparently, my forty-yard speed was the second-fastest lineman speed on the whole team.

The coaches tested our strength in the weight room as well, and I did great. I maxed my bench press at 340 pounds and pushed up 315 pounds three times. This wasn't considered exceptional strength, but I wasn't looking for exceptional; I was looking to make the team.

They called us in. We were all nobodies, and only a few would soon be somebodies. They called out names and allocated some to this group and others to that group. What group was I in? The coach went to talk to the other group first. He was out of hearing range, so I studied his body language. He finished with a nod and clapped his hands together. What the hell did that indicate? The group dispersed toward the locker room. A pair of the possible somebodies joked around as they practically skipped along. Crap! I knew they were on their way to get their new uniforms. All the sacrifices I paid, and my dream still dies? Not like this, not like this—hill gods, where the hell were you?

The coach walked over to our group and then looked down at his clipboard. He flipped through a couple of pages and then read off each name in a monotone voice. When he finished, he grinned. "Congratulations," he said, still monotone. "You're Florida Atlantic University's newest football players. You all made the team."

I made it! I freaking made it! I was a Florida Atlantic Fighting Owl! I was elated. Things in my life were looking great now. The defensive coach mentioned that I was a redshirt candidate.[8] I had finally achieved my dream. During this time of my life, I learned that anything is possible with persistence and sacrifice. "Luck is what happens when preparation meets opportunity."[9] My horrible choice of joining the Navy was vindicated at last.

---

8 College teams choose to put their players on a redshirt status when they feel the players' potential is best used in the future. During the first year, the player attends school, participates in practices, but they cannot compete in games. In exchange for foregoing their first season, they are allowed a fifth season of football and a fifth year of school.

9 This quote is attributed to Lucius Annaeus Seneca, who was an ancient Roman philosopher.

CHAPTER 4

From Cold to Gold

Held back in a prerun stance, the pack eagerly awaited the ready-set-go sequence. Our green, thin shorts and undershirts gave us no pardon from the bristling cold air. We were a group of silent geysers puffing steam into the still, crisp morning. The tension was churning into angst. We rocked back and forth in anticipation of the call.

The guy next to me leaned forward too much and stepped on the guy in front of him. A whispered shouting match ensued but was cut short when a drill instructor stepped in with an angry stare. Our run would begin at the top of the steep "Da Nang," a hill named after a deadly battle in the Vietnam War. I couldn't wait to stretch out my legs. We had been so cooped up the past week that I felt atrophy beginning to set in.

We had been bunched together like veal since we arrived at the Marine Officer Candidates School in Quantico, Virginia. The corralling first began when the bus door opened and a short drill instructor with laryngitis started barking a foreign language at us. I understood a few four-letter expletives. We collectively assumed that he was telling us to get off the bus.

From there on, the next four processing days were some of the most difficult. Officer Candidates School softened us up with sleep deprivation, shocked us with their screaming, and then overwhelmed us with extreme boredom. We were forced to either stand still or sit still. Talking was prohibited. We learned this rule when one staff member yelled at us. "Keep your nasty mouths shut, and stop clearing your disgusting throats!" Unable to speak for days made phlegm build up in the back of my throat.

While in line, we had to get uncomfortably close, or drill instructors would remind us to "get nut to butt."[10] When we weren't standing in line, we were jammed into child-sized desks or steel chairs and forced to sit up straight and stay awake as if we were school children in detention.

We all arrived in the civilian attire that the Marine recruiters instructed us to wear: khaki pants and short-sleeved polo shirts. The various colors and styles of our outfits clashed with the uniformity of the camouflage-green snow jackets they threw on us. It was only the first day, yet we were already beginning our transformation to look alike as Marines do.

Quantico in the winter was bad enough, but Officer Candidates School made it torture by keeping us still for long periods of time—their hidden curriculum. On our first night, we stood at attention[11] outside forever as the first snow of the year gently powdered us. In minutes, we were covered. Minutes after that, the gentle snow soaked through our clothes and bit into our bones. On day two, we sat outside half the day on our foldable camp stools[12] in the subfreezing temperature. This was the day that we had the first candidate in our platoon quit.

"I'd like to drop on request," he said to a Marine nearby.

"Seriously?" the other Marine said. "We didn't even start yet."

A few hours later, a candidate fell unconscious. Days without urinating or a having a bowel movement had poisoned his body—he had been too scared to request to use the head. The other weak-bodied and weak-minded candidates also began to drop like flies.

---

10 The term *nut to butt* means to stand so close that one's genitals are pressed against the other's butt. The phrase is no longer used in the military because it is politically incorrect and could be viewed as a type of sexual harassment.

11 *Attention* is a military stance where the individuals are silent with their hands pinned to their trouser seams, their backs straight, and their eyes locked in a forward stare.

12 A camp stool is a portable, foldable stool designed to attach to a backpack.

I had the same make-it-or-break-it motivation that had burned inside me during my twelve-minute run on the football tryout. The snow was ankle deep and provided as much traction as sugar sand. The Marine captain—our platoon commander—was in front of me, and his stride kicked up snow in my face. Was he a jerk or was he just a quirky runner? I could barely keep up with him. My face was covered in muddy slush, but he didn't give a crap that he was flinging snow, and he didn't give a crap about me or any other meathead behind him. It's not that he was a bad guy; as it turns out, he was a great man and did care about others. He just hated candidates.

Officer Candidates School in Quantico is an institution that hates candidates. The dominant ideology among drill instructors and supporting staff is something like this: "Candidates are nasty civilians who haven't proved anything and deserve nothing less than maltreatment. Heck, if they don't like it, then they can go home! We don't want their type anyway. We don't want quitters."

On this very first day of training, we were less than "pukes"; rather, we were the indigestion that builds up before a puke. As when I had tried out for football, I was once again a nobody trying to be a somebody.

The coniferous forest was made up of barren, gray pines sprouting out of freshly powdered, white hills. The desolate hills provided a natural amphitheater that reverberated our rhythm of squishy steps and laborious breathing, along with the other offbeat sounds of spitting, snorting, and grunting. I was dialed into the Marine captain's pace but wouldn't dare pass him. A few calm breathers behind me kept a steady pace. I found out later they were semi-professional runners. One of them ran track for Texas A&M and could run five kilometers in sixteen minutes, compared with the average twenty-eight-minute male runner. They couldn't pass me because I was practically on the Marine captain's heels.

The rest of the pack were one hundred yards back and clumped together. They may have been behind us, but none of them would dare fall out unless they had a heatstroke, because whoever fell out of the run would be considered weak and shunned. Pack pressure, as I referred to the conformity, was overall a good thing on runs because it kept you in the fight. No one wanted to be "that guy." If you went against the norm, you would mark yourself as the outsider, which was akin to blood in the water for the drill instructors.

The crystalized moisture was difficult to pull into my lungs, so I received less oxygen and became light-headed. I had no choice but to suck it up. I had promised myself before signing up that I would never give up. "You aren't going home unless you're in a hearse," I told myself. "I don't care if they saw your legs off at the knees and make you run through a cornfield. You will never quit. And you will never let anyone see physical weakness."

I held on to this credo throughout training. I never did quit, and I never did show weakness—I didn't even shiver. They wouldn't break me.

I used this first run as a mental pause where I could zone out. I secretly enjoyed the scenery as I pondered the challenge I was about to embark upon. I was preparing mentally for the worst of the worst. I looked into my well of fortitude, built with the fabric of hard-core experiences that I'd successfully completed. Knowing that I'd survived these would give me the confidence to make it through the rough road ahead.

I lowered myself deep into my well, where my peewee-league football moments, like the suicide sprints and that hot El Camino, resided. I could still hear the TWEET of the whistle and feel the blast of hot air from the car's heater. At the bottom of the well were my grandfather's and father's experiences that lived in me even then and still do now. They had been Marines in the two bloodiest wars of the twentieth century.

My grandfather, Papa, had been in the great battles of Peleliu, Midway, Guadalcanal, and a few other Pacific battles of World War II. Some of these battles had posted an 80 percent mortality rate. Dad had been an infantryman in Da Nang, Vietnam, where he'd endured fourteen months of heavy combat. It was a spectacular coincidence that the first hill I'd run at Officer Candidates School shared the name of a place where his ghost almost roamed. If Dad or Papa had been killed in action, I would never have been born. In a way, I was a manifestation of their survival. If they endured that bloody hell, then I could damn sure survive this. I was not going home unless I became a Marine officer.

I was warmed up now. I fell into a comfortable stride, and my lungs were wide open. I was relaxed for the first time since arriving. I suddenly and instinctively knew that I could hang on, no matter how long the run would be. Then we abruptly stopped. I did not realize that the run was over. I was puzzled, and my eyes darted about as I searched the area for an answer. The billboard digital clock displayed the hours in red while the minutes cycled through the seconds. It read 0:40 minutes, with the seconds cycling to the millisecond. It was over.

The Marine captain stopped running and walked off to the side. "There's no way that was forty minutes," I thought, looking around at the other runners. This has to be a joke. We just started. I was stunned for several moments before finally comprehending that we had indeed been running for forty minutes. It blew my mind! I had been mentally absent and in another place for the past five miles. Somehow, I had escaped time during the run. This was the first positive running experience. Running became a way for me to escape time and torture.

A chubby fellow candidate crossed the line with the last stragglers. He looked dazed and was walking off-balance. A team of Navy corpsmen[13] laid him down on the ground and pulled his trousers down to his ankles. He pleaded with the medical team not to shove the anal thermometer inside him. "Please, no. I'm okay now. Please, no!"

There was no arguing against the standard procedures for someone overheating. A few moments later, I heard him shout. I realized right then and there that they don't mess around here. Fall out from heat exhaustion, and they'll violate you with a thermometer nicknamed "The Silver Bullet."

On the night bus ride from JFK Airport in Washington, DC, to Officer Candidates School in Quantico, Virginia, I argued with a guy who claimed that it would never snow where we were located. As we went back and forth, I gazed past him, out the bus window at drifting snowflakes. The argument was over; unfortunately, my point was proved every day over the next week and reinforced throughout the entire training period. I don't remember a day without snow. Along with abundant snowfall, the ground remained frozen for most of the ten weeks we spent there. We literally hiked up and down

---

13 Navy corpsmen go along with Marines on all missions.

frozen hills. The drill instructors loved to use the cold to make us even more miserable. They would conveniently forget to fix vital amenities such as heat and hot water in our squad bay,[14] our living quarters.

After our first two weeks of freezing training, with temperatures ranging from ten to thirty degrees Fahrenheit,[15] our lead drill instructor calmly asked us a question. "Why didn't any of you smelly candidates tell me that we did not have hot water in our showers?" His calmness had a lick of sarcasm. It was far too calm for his usual demeanor. I'm *sure* that he had *no idea*. Yeah, right.

A few weeks later, he counseled us in the same tone, asking why on earth we didn't report the broken window inside our squad bay that had caused severe suffering. He must have overlooked the fact that it was twenty degrees inside! The nights were so cold that we had to draw our sleeping bags closed and leave a tiny hole for breathing. Waking up in the middle of the night to go pee was torture. Waking up wasn't too much of a problem, though, because we rarely slept that first month.

The worst cold torture took place after our breakfasts at 4:30 a.m. We ate with one hand on our knee and the other shoveling food into our mouth. "Aye, Gunnery Sergeant! Aye, Gunnery Sergeant! Aye, Gunnery Sergeant!" the candidate shouted back to the drill instructor, who was only six inches away but screaming into his ear. In a cynical way, I snickered because the poor candidate would have a mouthful of food and, as he shouted, the half-chewed food would fly everywhere, as if he were the Cookie Monster. The chow hall (cafeteria) sounded like a slaughterhouse. Candidates screamed, and drill instructors flipped trays and barked orders. I even heard a few growls followed by whimpers.

---

14 A squad bay is a large room with about eighty bunk beds, forty on each side, with a path down the middle. During certain times, the candidates stood in front of their racks, lined on both sides, and faced each other as the drill instructors ran up and down the middle path. The squad bays also encompassed the drill instructor hut and a restroom (head).

15 These were the fourth-coldest average temperatures in Quantico, Virginia, from records from weather-warehouse.com, dating back to 1976.

After this ordeal, we would stand outside at attention with our arms fully extended in front of us, holding our regulations directly in front of our faces. At times, I would sneak a peek over my book to watch some white birds that came to the river every morning, lethargically slogging through gray sludge on the banks of the frozen Potomac River. What type of bird could possibly survive such frozen hell? Who knows, but at least they got to move a little.

After about ten to twenty minutes of standing, we would get to march back to the barracks. The icy-cold, steel M16 rifles were a conduit that transferred the cold from the atmosphere directly into our bones. My fingertips would burn from the iciness. Once we got inside our sometimes-heated squad bay, our hands would quickly defrost, but this rapid change of temperature felt like acid pouring over my fingers. The expression that always came to mind was hell froze over.

I dredged through the waist-high mud and kept my rifle high and clean. In one memorable instance, a drill instructor found some mud jammed in one of the candidate's rifle barrel and then boomeranged it into the woods. Of course, this boomerang didn't come back, so the candidate ran after it, slipped on ice, and sledded down a frozen ravine, almost breaking a leg.

I was only a few miles into the four-mile endurance course before having to visit a few memories in my well of fortitude. My boots became muddy buckets of water. The swamp sucked in each step. Our combat gear was made up of camouflage utility uniforms, along with forty-pound assault packs, a belt with canteens and rifle cartridges, and a Kevlar helmet, and we held our M16s.

My breathing was strong from six weeks of this hell. I was fortified. I was strong, and there was nothing that was going to stop me. The five-mile endurance course was the hardest of all runs at Officer Candidates School. This run made a Spartan Race[16] look like a game of hopscotch. The course began with

---

16 Spartan Races are civilian outdoor obstacle course runs hosted by a company called Spartan. These races are marketed as incredibly difficult. The trail-type runs incorporate exciting activities such as running over crushed cars on fire, climbing up cargo nets, and crawling through mud. However, runners are not required to carry rifles; drill instructors are not present during the race; and participants do not undergo severe sleep deprivation for weeks prior to the event.

the double obstacle course to take the wind out of you. The o-course was a series of horizontal bars and a wall to pull yourself over and logs to run on and hurdle over, culminating with climbing a twenty-foot rope. We did this twice.

After the initial gut punch, we began the five-mile run. This hellish course covered the extreme portions of the Quantico-like terrain. You dragged yourself through various obstacles you had to conquer while the M16 rifle, which was strung over your shoulder, swung and smacked into just about everything.

Running down those Quantico hills was the minivacation. "Relax your hips and open your stride," a sergeant told me as I huffed and puffed beside him. My rifle was frozen to my hands. But, hey, at least I wasn't standing still. We were all completely spent from slogging through chest-high, thick mud and then having to climb up a small cliff or descend a steep ravine. I would run on pure adrenaline and the fear of failing.

The e-course culminated with the infamous Quigley obstacle. This was a courage test. Could a candidate remain calm while shimmying upside down and backward through ice-cold water and old barrels? I got to the beginning, and my canteens that were hooked on the back of my belt got hung up on the front lip of the barrel. I couldn't lie low enough to keep my face from rubbing against the top of the barrel. I felt the need to inform one of the drill instructors.

"My canteens are—"

He responded before I could finish. "I don't give a fuck!" He pushed me under. I got stuck and pushed my feet as hard as I could to jam my way though. Drill instructors tugged me out through the other side. As I gasped for air, I cleaned my rifle.

Another extremely difficult task at Officer Candidates School that nearly broke me was major sleep deprivation. The first week, I had racked up a total of four hours of sleep.

"Go to sleep, candidates," they'd tell us. "And oh, by the way, you have to do these twenty items before the morning."

My short-term memory became so bad that I would forget where I placed something only seconds earlier. I would set a flashlight on my bed, turn around to do something, and, seconds later, I would forget where it was. I would see a flashlight on the bed next to mine, so I would grab it, and moments later I'd hear the guy next to me. "Where's my flashlight?" he'd ask. I heard a few people say that. Things were too chaotic. I didn't know the difference between finding something I'd totally forgotten about and stealing someone else's stuff. Sleep deprivation had adverse effects on me, but some candidates fell way off base.

The drill instructor upended a footlocker, and several oranges rolled out in all directions. He chucked the footlocker at the wall and yelled. "What the hell is this, Candidate Skittles?"[17] I could feel the oxygen getting sucked from the room as if we were in a fire's backdraft. We stood in two lines facing each other in the standard squad bay—barracks with aligned bunks. I could barely stop myself from bursting into laughter. I clenched my butt together and sucked my cheeks in like a fish while staring at the candidate in front of me. He seemed to be struggling too; a few of his cheek muscles twitched as he fought back laughter. The moment of tension almost made me the center of attention.

The toughest challenge for me in my military career has been to hold a straight face while standing at attention or during other instances that require a stoic and still face. The key to success requires trusting the individual who is part of the joke or laugh. If he breaks, then you most definitely will. It is a moment of pure faith and trust. I can't even imagine what the consequences would have been if we had burst into laughter, as we so wanted to.

I struggled even more as the situation escalated. Stretching my eye to the left peripheral, I could see the drill instructor holding a black plastic plate. "You were eating Chinese food too?" he asked in a shout, as if someone had shot his favorite horse. I was blown away how anyone would have enough stupid courage to bring in some chicken chow mein when these monsters

---

17 "Skittles" was the nickname the drill instructors gave him after they caught him tasting the rainbow-colored candies during patrol training. The sea story is that when they caught him, each fingertip was a different color, and his lips were purple.

would ruin your day for even looking at them wrong. The thoughtless candidate replied with the wrong answer—funny, but wrong. "This candidate was hoarding oranges for the hike tomorrow, Gunnery Sergeant."

Candidate Skittles didn't last long. They would constantly ask him when his spaceship was coming for him. They rode his butt so hard that he eventually quit. In Officer Candidates School, the policy is that candidates will not be sent home unless they fail three academic tests, get hurt, or drop on request. It was all our choice to be there. They had perfected their methods of pressuring someone to leave though. Their next victim would usually be told to move to the "hot rack," which is the bed closest to the drill instructor's hut in the squad bay.

This nightmare experience changed my perspective on running. Runs became my only sanctuary from the constant pain. They warmed me up, helped me forget about time, and gave me space from the harassing drill instructors. Runs were also fun and motivating. My favorite were the platoon runs where we all chanted traditional Marine Corps cadences. The cadences are often politically incorrect, but exceptions are made because they've been sung for hundreds of years. Here is one of my favorites:

"Hey, Hey Captain (Whiskey) Jack"
Hey, hey Captain Jack
Meet me down by the railroad track
With a bottle in your hand
I'm gonna be a drinkin' man
A drinkin' man

Hey, hey Captain Jack
Meet me down by the railroad track
With a K-bar in your hand
I'm gonna be a stabbin' man

A stabbin' man
A drinkin' man

Hey, hey Captain Jack
Meet me down by the railroad track
With a bible in your hand
I'm gonna be a preachin' man

A preachin' man
A stabbin' man
A drinkin' man

Hey, hey Captain Jack
Meet me down by the railroad track
With a lady in your hand
I'm gonna be a lovin' man

A lovin' man
A preachin' man
A stabbin' man
A drinkin' man

Hey, hey Captain Jack
Meet me down by the railroad track
With a rifle in your hand
I'm gonna be a shootin' man

A shootin' man
A lovin' man
A preachin' man
A stabbin' man
A drinkin' man

Singing songs like this at the top of our lungs motivated us and taught us
how to control our breathing. To shout off a line of lyrics, one must take deep
breaths. With each cadence, we called upon the spirits of the generations of

Marines who sang the same songs before us. This was chilling and incredibly spiritual. While singing, I would often become overwhelmed with the thought of actually becoming a Marine like Papa and Dad. I would also be the first officer since the Bolenders began our Marine-service legacy in 1923.[18] The thought of becoming part of this legacy made me cry. You never had to hold back your tears on a run; they would simply fall, blending with the sweat on your face.

On April 27, 2007, I was commissioned as a second lieutenant in the US Marine Corps. My Officer Candidates School class 194 was the first to commission at the Marine Corps Museum in Quantico, Virginia. The museum has an exhibit for every major war the US Marine Corps has participated in. My two favorites here were the lifelike Vietnam and Peleliu portions. They're so realistic that the temperatures are set accordingly.

It is traditional for a Marine to have a friend, family member, or spouse pin on his or her new rank insignia. Dad pinned on one of my new gold second-lieutenant bars on my right shoulder in the Vietnam exhibit, and Papa pinned on the other gold bar on my left shoulder in the Peleliu exhibit. Tears could not be concealed on that day when I became part of our legacy. As this very regal ceremony played out, my brain was shouting, "I freakin' did it! I successfully went from cold to gold!"

---

18 Including me, there have been a total of seven Bolender Marines and two sailors in the Bolender family (I counted myself as both). Since 1923, we have served in World War II, Vietnam, and Afghanistan.

CHAPTER 5

Running a Long Distance from Home

"**A**re you a Marine, sir?" the waiter asked me after he saw my USMC shirt.

He rolled up his sleeve to unveil his tattoo of the eagle, globe, and anchor, the Marine Corps symbol. "I'm a reservist," he said proudly. "Semper fi."[19]

He was a Marine sniper, the best of the best. We had both been in Afghanistan at the same time during 2010. That had been my first Afghanistan tour and his fourth. He described some of the places he'd fought in, and I deduced that my unit had controlled the military aircraft that supported him. Where he fought had been one of the deadliest hot spots in western Afghanistan at the time. When I told him that I was a tactical air controller who had helped him get air support in Afghanistan, he froze, and his face lit up.

His eyes moistened up and his voice crackled with emotion as he explained. "We called you guys our guardian angels because of how you saved our asses all the time. There were so many aircraft hovering over us that they looked like little black dots, so we called it pepper sky. I constantly thought about how miraculous it was that those planes didn't collide and how on earth they managed *not to* drop a bomb on my ass. You saved my life!"

He offered me one of his hog's teeth, a wooden tooth necklace a sniper receives when he has a confirmed kill on an enemy sniper—a rare feat.

---

19 *Semper fi*, short for *semper fidelis*, is a universal motto used by Marines that means "always faithful."

"Without you guys, I wouldn't have three of these." He told me that the last time we'd saved him was an extremely close call. He'd shot and killed a sniper but gave away his position in the process. Dozens of combatants had swarmed his position and bogged him down. He'd been convinced that he was going to die. Within six minutes, the enemy had closed within six hundred feet.

Suddenly, a curtain of bombs had rained down from the heavens. Clusters of smoke and sand had puffed out and incinerated the target, and seconds later the cracking sounds followed. He had been what is known as *danger close*; any closer, and he would've been within the kill radius.[20] He'd felt the heat from those aircraft glide over him. The air support had taken six minutes.

He repeatedly thanked me and began to weep. We hugged as he continued to thank me. Here was this bad-ass sniper telling *me* that I had saved his life. In moments like this, you have that deep, abiding feeling that somehow your life has made a difference.

I was sure to tell junior Marines this story, saving it for those special times when they felt as if their job had little purpose. Sometimes they lose sight of the end result of their efforts. We all have moments like that, mainly because we rarely ever see the faces of those we save. The waiter, Staff Sergeant Emry's wife showed up within a few minutes and comforted him. I could tell that she'd been through this many times before. I'm pretty sure that he had major posttraumatic stress disorder, and she knew just how to steer him away from the conversation about his experiences.

My service in Afghanistan wasn't dangerous. My battle was against stress. Once again, runs became my escape from a chaotic world.

The temperature was well over one hundred degrees at Camp Leatherneck, Afghanistan, but I needed this run to cool down. My sweat evaporated instantly and left behind lines of salty grime on my face like

---

20 A kill radius is determined by the type of bomb or ordinance and the radius at which all things will be killed. *Danger close* refers to the distance determined to be safe, but the margin for error on behalf of the pilots could result in casualties.

high-water marks on the shore. I was arid and scorched, so my eyebrows had no function, no sweat to divert. My throat was parched and leathery.

I had needed to break away from my work space, which was a kitchenette-sized, dark room lit by dozens of computer monitors. The operating module was dark but so alive—a steel, green box made out of a truck trailer and wired with '70s technology. The giant machines, racks, switches, and ribbon wires were less capable than a first-generation iPod. Their abilities compared better with the original Nintendo game console.

Inside this analogue monster, four other Marines and I were responsible for the tactical air control of every military airplane and the integration of bombs and guided rockets in the entire western portion of Afghanistan.[21] Imagine yourself in a 747, and a thousand feet below you is a missile. We also had to control all the air-refueling missions. The airspace was so saturated and things were so chaotic that we made the job of a civilian air-traffic controller in charge of the busiest commercial airport seem as relaxing as a cashier job at a candle shop.

Our cramped space reminded me of the US Stock Exchange—that is, manic and chaotic but, at the same time, methodical and controlled. Radios squelched and blared the voices of the pilots and controllers, somewhat similar to a 911 dispatch center, except this was in a war zone. This is what we did, in a sense. We would receive the air-support mission and get the jets to support the troops ASAP.

The room was too busy and loud. It was almost impossible to speak to the person sitting right next to you. We were all too busy talking to aircraft and chatting with a dozen other military agencies over our headsets, phones, and computers. We were forced to exchange information with yellow Post-it sticky notes. A typical message would read something like, "This jet's mission has changed. Send him to this latitude and longitude immediately." When that failed, I would scream, shake the person, or throw something. You did

---

21 This is by no means suggesting that four of us did the entire mission. Thousands of Marines supported this function. Generator mechanics, electricians, truck drivers, cybertechnicians—the list goes on and on. The four in this operating module refer to those who were actually talking and directing the air traffic.

whatever it took to manage one of the most dangerous airspaces since World War II, before the era of controllers.[22]

It was 2010 and ten years since my first overseas deployment aboard the USS *Harry S. Truman*. Now, I was overseas again, this time at Camp Leatherneck, a Marine Corps base that was adjoined to a British air base called Camp Bastion. This 1,600-acre square was right in the middle of the Registan Desert, just north of Helmand Province, Afghanistan. The road surface around Camps Bastion and Leatherneck was hard-packed sand topped with a thin layer of powdery, talcum-like dust. Moondust, as we called it, was soft and forgiving on the knees. It was also a big pain in the ass. It silted our clothes, electronics, and pillowcases. Anything white turned beige. Moondust got in my ears and powdered my nose hairs. It was too fine to completely wash out of your mouth. Instead, you would wind up grinding it between your teeth anytime you were outside breathing it into your lungs.

Moondust was a mechanic's and pilot's worst nightmare. It put a major strain on all machines by getting inside the gears and sticking to the grease. When it came to flying, helicopter pilots hated to land in the crap. The helicopter's rotor downwash would stir the dust to the point of zero visibility. The horizon, a main reference for any type of pilot, would disappear. Pilots could easily become discombobulated to the point where they would lose sight of what was up or down. Without a cockpit view, they relied on their instruments. If the terrain wasn't completely flat, they could roll over. They were extremely vulnerable to enemy fire. It was one big mess, as if war weren't messy enough.

From a runner's perspective, the moondust was mostly a good thing, unless it got windy or there were too many trucks. The majority of the trucks at Leatherneck were contracted out by Pakistanis who decorated their trucks with insane regalia like nothing I'd seen before. They were painted to resemble exactly what a belly dancer would look like if she were a dump truck. Pendants, chains, and streamers dangled from their sides and front bumpers. That was probably how they got their name; everyone called them

---

22 Britain had controllers, but this was a nuance in the world and was a scarce resource.

"jingle trucks." The rest of the trucks—every square inch—were decorated with multicolored gems and other Eastern religious thingies. These bedecked beasts were recognized as kings of the roads in this jungle. If they weren't running up and down the roads carrying supplies, they would be transporting sand or helping build roads.

These trucks were also obnoxiously loud, and their presence was always stressful because they robbed any activity, especially my runs, of all peace. Avoiding them was almost impossible. The base where I was stationed was growing by leaps and bounds almost overnight. These trucks fed that growth, so they never stopped coming from outside the base or leaving to deliver something. The drivers must have been crazy or paid a high wage to drive on those IED-littered roads off base.

A line of jingle trucks approached, and I hopped to the side of the road. I could shield myself from the dust of a single truck, but a convoy brought a cloud of moondust that was too big to steer clear of. In fact, it was enough dust to choke a camel. This train of road kings had trapped me, holding me captive in their gritty fog from hell for at least a few hundred yards.

I was so hot, and now we were adding tons of dust. I could barely breathe, but I tried to remain positive. These runs under very hot conditions always seemed to help me burn the stress off my soul. It was a process that I was familiar with but never really understood.

Before I knew it, the air changed again. This time, I was breathing in a dingy haze caused by the trash fires that lined the road. I could not fathom how the eerie-looking man throwing trash into the white-hot incinerator did his job. As I jogged past, he stared at me with a red glare, a fire in his eyes. He appeared like a true-to-life zombie. Something was inhumane about his job. I imagined him getting sick from the toxins, and, instead of treating him, someone would just toss him in the fire and then replace him the following week.

Countless poverty-stricken men probably would have taken the gig in a flash. The job was so faceless that no one would even realize if there was a new guy. Nobody around the base would get close enough to the dirty fire to actually see the face of the zombie who manned it. Sadly, the next guy would soon look just as dirty and sick as the old one, and the cycle would continue. I held my breath for about a minute and then gasped. Who knows what hellish crap was in that air? I didn't care because I needed this run mentally. I'd deal with the physical consequences later.

Out of the haze, I could barely see that I was about to cross over from Camp Leatherneck to Camp Bastion located on the other side of the skinny corridor. The road narrowed to the width of an early twentieth-century bridge. Ahead was another convoy that hurried toward me. I attempted to cross to the other side, but still another convoy approached from the opposite direction. The corridor was definitely too narrow for the beasts and me, so I hopped onto the side berm.

It felt as if I was stuck in a knee-high kiddie-ball pit. I sunk in, and the trucks began blowing by. They were close. A complete moondust whirlwind assaulted me, causing an absolute brownout. As I waited for the convoy to pass, I thought about our pilots. How the hell could anybody fly in this? They must have been crazier than the jingle truckers.

I couldn't see at all, so I knew there was no way they would be able to see me. Truck after truck clanked, clunked, and chugged by just a few feet away. I was caught in a dusty eddy and running in place—stuck in a very awkward and somewhat-dangerous place. Ugly thoughts ran through my head. A single trip or misstep, and I would be turned into a bloody clump like cat shit in a kitty-litter box.

Thank God there was a lull. This would've been an embarrassing way to die. I envisioned my wife being notified of my death. The Marine would pull out a poster-board picture of the clown-like truck. My wife would begin weeping but pause to ask a question.

"What the hell is that?"

The Marine would somberly bow his head. "Ma'am, this is what killed him. He suffered death by jingle truck. It was all so horrible. We were barely able to identify his body."

My wife would continue crying but be really confused, for deep down, she would have the crazy urge to laugh out loud. My death would be soon forgotten, but the jingle trucks would continue their runs.

These dusty, dangerous, and obnoxiously loud trucks, and even the toxic air, never kept me from the sanctuary I'd find in my runs. Others had their release; this was mine.

A 210-day deployment brings stress to Marines, either from the job or from affairs back home. Some would do their job with ease and then come home to find out that their wife or husband cheated on them. Others would have a healthy home front but blow a fuse on the job. No matter what, leaving home, a spouse, a family, or a pet for seven months adds stress to your life. We all had to find ways to escape. Some read books, some worked out, and some wrote letters. I ran.

Most Marines found relief in creativity and humor, which goes against the stoic image that a lot of people associate with Marines. One of my favorite funny moments was when a fellow Marine complained one day that someone stole his instant coffee. He was furious and would not let up. He rummaged through boxes and bins and tossed gear all over. He never found his coffee but berated a few subordinates to ruffle a bunch of feathers.

The next morning, those whom he had confronted decided to greet him and his crew with a makeshift, unofficial Starbucks cafe. You want coffee, eh? We'll bring you the whole freakin' coffee shop. They strung strands of lighting inside the tent, and then they turned the other lights off to set a calm and dim ambience. They made showcase counters out of discarded cardboard. In place of the pastries, they put muffins and candy from a Meal, Ready-to-Eat.[23] They drew the Starbucks logo on white Styrofoam cups. These Marines then tied their camouflage shirts around their waists and took orders as if they were professional baristas. They made hot coffee and lattés from authentic Starbucks coffee grounds and chocolate milk, along with other concoctions they scrounged from care packages.

That night, the whole crew took a break from their stressful daily life and pretended to be in America at their local coffeehouse sipping on delicious

---

23 A Meal, Ready-to-Eat, or MRE, is a field ration that comes in a sealed, thick, plastic bag with a main meat or vegetarian course and is complemented by side items such as crackers, candy, milkshake mix, and various other treats. It's high in calories and meant to provide enough calories for a man for an entire day.

treats. They took a moment to experience a surreal suspension of disbelief where they imagined their lives to be normal. The setting and ambience were weirdly similar to the real deal. It took on the life of a coffee shop. People were having intellectual conversations to soft music, and everyone was content for a while. It was indeed a classic moment.

Unfortunately, our "Starbucks: Afghanistan"[24] was knocked down the next day when the grumpy villain, who was the butt of the joke, directed subordinates to get rid of it. Cardboard was ripped apart, and leftovers were pillaged. It was sad to see it go.

Most Marines blew off steam by lifting weights. Some smoked cigarettes and played the guitar. The gamers got lost in their virtual realms. As long as Marines had their toys, they were good. One time, a high-ranking officer ordered that all televisions be confiscated from our lounges. These lounges and our televisions served as a type of decompression chamber where we could unwind from the high stress. The officer permitted only Marine Corps doctrinal books and other similar war-related reading. What a dweeb.

I decided to keep my stress at bay by eliminating frequent communication with my family. My wife and I decided to temporarily forget about each other. We loved each other, and I adored my kids more than anything in this world, but being gone and trying to concentrate on such a difficult mission was too much to balance. We didn't cut ties altogether; we just talked every couple of weeks as opposed to every day.

These are the types of sacrifices service members make often. For some, the sacrifices are much greater than this. I missed out on 210 days of life. I will never experience my youngest child's third birthday, my oldest child's ninth birthday, my wife's thirtieth birthday, and our marriage anniversary.

My job took 100 percent of my focus and intelligence. During my first few days in Afghanistan, I was 99 percent confident that I would either quit or be fired. I had two weeks to assume responsibility for the safety, routing, and deconfliction of all military flights; all ordinances delivered; all air-to-air refueling; direction of unmanned aerial systems; integration of bombs and

---

24 Disclaimer: This makeshift Starbucks was by no means authorized or sponsored by Starbucks Corp.

rockets to weave safely through aircraft; and dozens of other similar tasks. We coordinated every square grid of the airspace, and it was insane.

Many years later, I learned that during my time in Afghanistan, our military was at the pinnacle of its tactical air support and airspace saturation for the Afghanistan War. We controlled 450 aircraft per day, managed about five million pounds of fuel a day, and coordinated safe resolutions of one in-flight emergency per week.

I had been trained for about nine months on how to do my job, but on my first day, I was completely lost. I knew that those blips on the radar screen were aircraft, but I didn't know how we were supposed to control them. I would look around a crowded control room and think, "Who else is helping us do all this?"

Adding to this angst was the expectation that I was supposed to be the supervisor of the air-traffic section in two weeks. So many aircraft were in the sky at any given time that some had to wait over an hour for a piece of airspace. Priority went to the air-to-ground support that was requested by troops on the ground. I had no idea that, in seven months, we would control over 43,000 missions and, on one day, 107 air-to-ground support requests. I had no idea I was capable of this role. The guy I was replacing was responsible for training me. I just kept thinking that he would surely come to a realization that I was not capable of this kind of work. I was sure that once they found out that I was a dumb ass, I would be cast into a lesser job with the other incompetent or "slow" people. I was terrified.

An officer's reputation is everything. It's like his business brand; it's what makes or breaks him. I faced being cast aside and labeled a dummy and poor leader. I began to concentrate on trying to learn this more than anything else in my entire life up to that point. Surely, if I listened closely and focused intently, I could learn enough from my teacher to at least become a mediocre leader.

I would come off a four-hour watch period and be so frustrated with myself for not learning fast enough. It seemed as if my predecessor and teacher would pick up on this fear and heavily critique and correct me. Then I'd go away feeling worse than ever. It was a self-defeating cycle of the worst kind, and I couldn't break free of it. I remember telling myself that I might fail. Up until then, I'd never actually thought about accepting defeat, but I didn't want someone to die because of me.

I was taught to "deal with it" by running out to the corner of our lot and beating a tire with a sledgehammer. After I spent a week of dealing with it this way, my hands were blistered and banged up from overusing the sledgehammer. This got old fast. I needed a lifeline, something or someone to bring me to something better than a tire. This method did a great job of ridding me of much of the frustration, but it was not fun or enjoyable in any way. Wasn't there anything that could be both fun and a stress reducer? At that point in my life, runs worked well to get rid of the stress but were rarely fun.

One day, Mark Lee, a UK Royal Air Force sergeant, asked me to run a 10K. I enjoyed running only a couple of miles at a time, so I blew him off.

Finally, he cornered me. "Oh bollocks,[25] you're going to man up and go for a run with me tomorrow," he said in his heavy British accent.

The next day, I accepted his challenge to "man up." We chugged along, and I kept checking my GPS watch to make sure that we were holding the exact pace agreed on. Our first run was farther than I'd ever run before, so I wanted to make sure that I expended just the right amount of energy as I ran along. I suspected that Mark was getting frustrated at how I was tethered to the device. Apparently, I was poking at one of his pet peeves. I asked him if he used a GPS, and he immediately took the opportunity to dismantle the concept of running to an exact pace measured with a smart device.

"The GPS limits you to the minute details of a plan. Running is about freedom, and you are staring at your watch instead of enjoying the view of this crappy desert. That machine is a sodding leech, and you are letting it suck the runner's blood out of you. Use a watch to look at your pace at the end. While you are running, you need to learn to listen to your body and pay attention to what is a natural pace and stride for it. You will learn that this style is much better than being a GPS slave."

---

25 *Bollocks* is a British slang word that means "testicles" ("Oh balls").

We ran many sunsets together in this dusty shit hole. Running took us away from the brain-cooker '70s computer box and gave us a break from our coworkers. We could talk in private, complain about anything, tell each other about family members, and talk about what we loved in life—and we could gossip. Mark took me under his wing and showed me the way to survive the distance and how to love it.

The base was on a grid-square design, so we would choose a new road to travel each time, just to keep things different. The scenery was a bit bland everywhere, but sunsets promised beauty over this war-torn country. The base was a small, developing city, so things changed often, keeping the journeys interesting. We ran by a charred supply depot that had burned down. This had once been a large supply hub, holding 90 percent of the spare parts for equipment for the base. The day it went up in flames was a bit scary. We ran out of our operating modules and saw a series of fireballs swoop up into the air and burn out into puffs of smoke in the sky. It looked like an air-refueling tanker aircraft (C-130) had exploded on the ground. But we would have known if this had happened because we controlled them. This didn't make sense. Had we been attacked? Minutes later, we got the news about the depot. The investigation determined that the fire was most likely caused by a cigarette butt that someone didn't properly extinguish.

Out in front of the charred depot sat a fleet of contractor trailers that held green sod. The drivers, who were all contractors, had decent cars parked in their driveways. Marine units had cars to get around base as well, but their cars weren't anywhere as nice as these almost-new ones. The contractors also washed their cars regularly and watered their grass weekly. The other Marines and I were told to turn off the water while we soaped and shampooed, but these guys used up plenty of water to keep their cars and lawns looking good.

Mark's and my runs were all unique explorations. On the Camp Bastion side, the Brits made some great-smelling food. Running hungry to the smell of cooking meat is a primitive experience. The scent would get into my blood and deliver adrenaline to prepare me to hunt down an animal. Great Britain cared more about the details and morale of their men than did the United

LITTLE RUNS BIG WORLD

States regarding their own men. I had decided that the reason the Brits' food smelled so good was because they put love into cooking it.

We spent one hundred times as much on our food, but contractors who didn't really even know us prepared it. Maybe we'd put a little love in the food, and it would taste better if we cooked it for ourselves. The Brits also had social spaces such as coffee shops, Indian-curry stands, and pizza stands. They had a Green Bean coffee shop that served better coffee than our unofficial Starbucks. The Brit side of the base was calming and fun to run through. They were less serious than Americans but equally professional and dedicated to the mission. The only paved roads were on the Camp Bastion side. On one day, a few Brits were skateboarding with a rope attached to a jeep. This would never fly on the US side.

Camp Bastion is also where we staged the HIMARS launchers.[26] These were guided rocket systems that could hit a target from over thirty miles away with extreme accuracy in any weather condition. They didn't miss, and we used them like a rib shack uses wet naps. They shot off every half hour or so, and each one guaranteed a kill. As we ran beside these, we were reminded that this war was real. What we did was real. People would die, and out there was chaos. We chatted about how many of these rockets we'd cleared the sky for. The blast-off thrusts motivated both of us.

I came to know Camps Leatherneck and Bastion quite well. I knew where the good smells came from. I chased many dusty sunsets while on ten-mile runs. These run journeys placed my stress in the shadows. These 210 days were about being away from home while doing a stressful job, but they were also about me finding my running spirit. This spirit taught me that I could run farther than before. I ran my first half marathon out there. This dirty base is where I became a distance runner, and this transformed me. I also succeeded in doing one of the most stressful jobs in the world. We never had any aircraft collide. We set the record for the amount of time air support was

---

26 The M142 high-mobility artillery-rocket system (HIMARS) is a US light-multiple rocket launcher mounted on a standard US Army medium tactical-vehicle truck frame.

delivered. Plus, we managed a half billion gallons of fuel and coordinated fifty thousand missions. I did a job that I knew I wasn't really good enough to do. But so many men and women were depending on me. How could I fail them? I ran farther than I'd ever imagined I would. I had grown.

We all remember our milestones, our first incredible experiences. This was my first relationship with a running route and the first time I would ever miss an environment such as being with a family member or close friend. I grew attached to those jingle trucks, that filthy air, and, above all, the release of stress and glory of a journey. This route was a sanctuary that I built one step at a time. I realized that I could actually love a space and environment. It hurt a bit to leave something that did so much for me. These long-distance, dusty runs brought a new depth to my well of fortitude that was deeper than my peewee-league El Camino and my Officer Candidates School.

Nobody will ever really appreciate what you do during times and places like this. Only you really know—you and the other Marines who shared the experience. Before leaving that extraordinary place, Camp Leatherneck, I learned that I would have to leave all the experiences there. If you bring them home with you and expect people to thank you or recognize what you did, it will grow into a chip on your shoulder. The sooner you get rid of it, the better off you'll be. Just let it go.

All Marines who went to Camp Leatherneck, or anyplace like it, exposed themselves to dangers and saw and heard things beyond what any normal person should ever experience. Captain Moon spoke to a detachment of eighty-seven Marines in the Tactical Operations Center before they left Afghanistan. He told us that we did the impossible by controlling the most chaotic airspace. This success gave the troops on the ground the air support they desperately needed. He reminded us that we saved lives every day and to bask in that glory. But he cautioned us to leave our egos in Afghanistan, because nobody will possibly understand just how important we were.

"Do not expect the credit you think you deserve. Wipe off the chip on your shoulder," he told us.

Most military men and women discover this on their own.

CHAPTER 6

Join the Club

"Would you like to have dinner after the run?" the guy said to me in a Facebook message.

"Wow, that would be nice!" I replied.

"Sounds cool, man!" the guy said.

I had just joined my first running club only a few days before and was already meeting new people. I wanted to continue running but needed to find a replacement for the grumpy Brit I ran with in Afghanistan. What better way than to join a club?

For some reason, I looked forward to running in a pack of strangers brought together by their love of running. Perhaps it was because, with strangers, there's no judgment or jokes about past failures or successes. The only thing that exists is the pure, unadulterated joy of running.

I had always enjoyed running in large formations of Marines, so this new running group would be great. There was one club on Facebook that seemed like a bunch of fun. They were out of Fort Lauderdale, so I would be able to join them during my visits in the summer. I was excited to be part of this new subculture of running. I could join a bunch of clubs all over and run with them whenever I visited that area.

The first run came around, and I began to get that feeling of exhilaration. The guy from Facebook laid out our course. We would start along the palm tree–lined Las Olas Boulevard, which would take us through the ritzy canal neighborhood where each mansion has a zillion-dollar yacht moored to its dock. These yachts primarily served as beautiful status symbols rather than actual seafaring vessels. Once through the million-dollar mile, we would run over a bridge that spans the sparkling-blue Intracoastal Waterway and brings us right to the Fort Lauderdale Strip.

"We'll see if we want to go farther when we get to the beach," the Facebook guy said in another post.

You can't go wrong with a beach run!

I arrived at the rendezvous point, where a football team–sized cluster huddled in a circle. I was a bit outside my comfort zone as the stranger plebe. The circle was closed. How would I break in? I didn't want to draw attention but had no choice except to walk on up and say hello. I was very familiar with new-guy awkwardness because the military constantly changes your job and moves you around the world, placing you through an endless cycle of resetting your professional and social identities. No matter how many times I experienced this change, I never got used to it, and it never got easier.

I wanted to fit in, so I made sure to show up wearing my short, green long-distance running shorts that the British flight sergeant would wear; they didn't even go down to midthigh. At some point, I realized that I actually enjoyed this style of minimalist clothing and eventually quit making fun of the Brit for his trunks.

The leader stood in the center and briefed us on our course. Thunder rumbled about twelve seconds away. That meant it was roughly ten to fifteen miles away, at least according to the scientific method most of us had learned in the third grade. The leader was in midsentence when I caught his eye. He stopped to introduce me to the group as the new member. They opened up the circle, and I joined their huddle. I noticed that most of the runners wore old T-shirts and normal shorts—nothing too professional. In fact, I was the only one in nice shoes and those long-distance short-shorts.

The awkwardness drifted away as I realized they weren't professional runners. No one cared what anyone else wore. These guys were all here to run and maybe hang out later. Some of the members talked about eating dinner afterward.

"Yeah, that's what we usually do. We work hard and then reward ourselves with twice as many calories than we burned off," I thought while listening.

Regardless, the idea of running with a pack and possibly scoring a running buddy was attractive to me. As we stretched, I noticed that only men had attended, and then I saw two men holding hands. I began to suspect that this was a gay-male running club. "That explains the dinner invites," I thought as we stretched. The situation became awkward again. My angst did not come from my indisposition of gays; rather, I was insecure about how they would accept me as the textbook, clean-cut, heterosexual Marine.

I began to have conflicting thoughts again. It's obvious that I'm in the military, and they will think that I made a mistake by showing up. They'll immediately believe that I'm a homophobe. They'll assume that I share the outlook of the military, which up till recently has been the least tolerant institution in the world of the LGBT community. They'll think I have a problem. They'll reject me!

By the time we finished stretching, I was convinced that everyone would hate me as soon as they learned that I was not gay. Of course, this was all in my head. The part about my making a mistake was true, but I had decided to stick with it and prove a point: the fact that this was a gay club didn't matter to me.

Before we could even get started, I began obsessing over what I was wearing. The craziness in my head started up again. Maybe I'm sending the wrong message by wearing the least amount of clothing of anyone in the group.

I was lost. I didn't know the social norms of this group, so I finally just decided to keep my mouth shut and run; after all, that *is* what I came to do. The aspect that I was obviously a "straight fish" out of water would eventually lead to an inspirational discussion that would develop into a wonderful running friendship.

The thunderstorm began with a light shower. A few gusts whooshed through the nearby trees, and palm leaves rattled. The scent of rain reminded me of the mildew stench in a dank, cheap hotel. I started off with the leading group. About a half mile into the run, the sky opened up and dumped buckets of cool water on us all. The thunder boomed overhead. We were in a full-fledged thunderstorm, and I didn't see anybody slow down or turn around.

The ballistic lightning reminded me that we are all mortals. Lightning electrocution is a freaky way to die because you have no way of knowing that it's about to strike you, and when it does, you won't even realize it. The speed of the lightning strike nails you before you can see it or get out of the way—before you can even process what has happened. One second I would be running, and the next I would be gone—literally in a flash.

The street gutters alongside Las Olas Boulevard became fast-flowing, white-water creeks. The white squall was now masking the view of those beautiful houses and boats. The entire environment had changed within moments, giving this little run a whole-new vibe. The run was no longer about the views; it was about not getting struck by lightning.

I caught up to a guy who had been just a few steps ahead of me for the past few minutes. I still felt insecure, so I stayed quiet. He introduced himself right away and asked me what branch of the military I was in. He had either seen my Facebook posts, or my so-called military look was way more obvious than I realized. Our conversation carried on for the next four miles until the end. We had an excellent heart-to-heart talk amid background booms, whistling winds, tree rattles, and cars swishing and splashing.

During this talk, we were both pseudoambassadors of our communities. I talked about the military culture, and he asked how *we* perceived gays. I made it clear that Marines look the same but share very different political, religious, and socio viewpoints. I felt the need to hammer home the point that the Marines and other service members cannot be accurately generalized—we deal with inaccurate stereotypes too. Our conversation was one that most Americans should have at some point in their lives.

We had a great talk about how the military had just recently repealed the ignorant and prejudiced "Don't Ask, Don't Tell" policy that barred gays from the military and forced service members to lie about their sexual orientation. I wanted him to know that I fully supported gay rights and their service to our nation. I told him how those who were bitter about it in the

Marine Corps would get over it and begin to embrace the fact that a Marine is a Marine no matter what his or her sexual preference is.

He talked about the struggles of being gay and being married twenty years ago when society shunned his lifestyle. He brought up how running has been there for him through struggles, through his ups and downs. For him, the running club was another way of bringing the gay community together.

I shared a story with him of something that had recently taken place. As an officer, I was a member of a group that had to tell other Marines that we could no longer discriminate against gays. When the "Don't Ask, Don't Tell" policy was repealed, our company's leadership and all other Marine Corps units were ordered to train everyone on the new changes and how they would affect our professional environment. We brought in the company of about eighty Marines and gave them a quick spiel about the matter. They all already knew everything we were going to say, but we still had to go through the new guidelines.

After the lecture, hands went up and several questions were raised. Someone began to ask a question. "What if we see two homosexuals—"

The commanding officer cut him off. "Um, we can't use that phraseology anymore. We must call them"—he paused, and a Marine standing nearby whispered something in his ear, then he continued—"the gays."

The Marine continued on with his question. "Okay, let's say the gay, or whatever, is making out with his boyfriend, or whatever, at the Marine Corps Ball."

The commanding officer gave a decent answer. "You would do the same as if you saw your buddy making out with some girl at the Marine Corps Ball." The answer was obvious, and the silence that ensued made the question seem stupid and lifeless.

We all knew what the answer to that question would be, but it wasn't about the question or the answer. It was about what would be acceptable language and treatment of gays going forward. This was totally up to our leadership; for once, our leadership did the right thing on the matter. They went about doing it in a clumsy way but with good intentions. They didn't have much of a choice.

Another officer chimed in with a good point that affirmed the new norm. "How many of you were in Afghanistan?" Half the room raised their hands. "How many of you served with the British?" The hands went back up. "We worked with them, showered in the same heads with them, and slept in the same tents as them. What if I told you that one-third of them were gay? Now tell me if or why that mattered."

Silence dominated the room. Silence was the perfect answer. At last, stupidity was silenced. For the first time since I joined the military in 1998, it was not okay or acceptable to refer to gays as fags or homos.

As I shared this story with my new running buddy, we began to form a friendship that still lives on today. When I visit my hometown, I usually call to see if he is available for a run. We always pick up our discussions where we had left off. Society, too, was changing so rapidly that each time we ran again, another piece of legislation had passed in favor of gay civil rights.

Our first meeting was right after the repeal of "Don't Ask, Don't Tell." The next occurred after the Department of Defense recognized gay marriage and granted those service members the same rights and benefits as heterosexuals. The Department of Defense and the military recognized gay marriage years before all fifty states did! Our next run was after the Supreme Court's ruling to legalize gay marriage in all fifty states.

Since I had first joined that running club, America had undergone major social and political changes. People with ridiculous concerns were finally silenced. It was never about whether gay rights and gay marriage were right or wrong. This was all about what would be the norm, what would be acceptable in our society. For the first time in America, our government could no longer limit the rights of citizens based on their sexual orientation.

CHAPTER 7

Back to the Desert, from the Desert

After seven long months in Afghanistan, I returned home to my family in Yuma, Arizona. My wife and two children greeted me wearing "Team Bolender" shirts and smothered me with hugs and kisses. It was time to bring my family back into my heart. Soon, things got back to normal, and the recent deployment seemed in the distant past.

Six months after returning, I was promoted to captain and became the company commander in charge of 103 Marines. My good friend, Captain Collins, became second in charge, acting as the company executive officer. For me, the most exciting part of being the detachment commander was leading formation runs. I led our group from the front, abreast with the Marine holding our platoon's detachment guidon. I picked the course and set the pace.

Our first group run as a detachment was one of the high points of my career and possibly the low point for a few of the men. Those who were grotesquely out of shape always avoided formation runs at all costs, and some of these *scammers* in the detachment were higher-ranking Marines.

I heard weak excuses, such as having to pick up the wife from work or preparing for such-and-such inspection. I didn't have the energy to play their games, so I would take note of their weak leadership and use it as ammunition on their next evaluation. Either way, they had to pay the piper.

Our first run served to oust the out-of-shape Marines in order to send a signal that poor fitness would not be tolerated. Before I took command,

I kept my thoughts to myself about how many of our high-ranking enlisted Marines were totally out of shape and falling away from the minimum standards of the Marine Corps. My predecessor had made an exception for these guys because they were good at their jobs. The problem I had was that all Marines are held to these standards the Marine Corps calls the "whole Marine"—that is, one who carries him- or herself professionally and, most importantly, stays in good physical shape. I had to weed out those who were not leading by example.

All Marines had a responsibility to maintain good physical shape and appearance, and any leader who failed to do this was guilty of watering down our standards and placing our teams at risk in combat situations. Often, Marines will realize the error of their ways and correct themselves after drifting out of line. Of course, everyone should get a second chance. I was more concerned about those who'd been in a slovenly condition for years, trying to avoid the truth about their condition.

Our route was the 2.5-mile circuit that we called the Gun Loop. My plan was to expose the grotesquely out-of-shape Marines by setting an exaggerated slow pace. It would be obvious that the Marines who fell out were physically inept. A mother pushing her baby in a stroller would easily pass us. We went so slow that a few Marines in front complained about their knees hurting from holding back. I chose to run us at 6:00 a.m. so that the temperature would be in the high sixties—perfect for any short run.

Off we went! In less than fifty feet, one Marine tumbled to the pavement and hurt his knee, so he was released to see the corpsman. In less than a quarter of a mile, roughly three minutes of shuffling, we had a couple of Marines bail and hop off to the side because they felt light-headed and sick or vomited. They probably figured that the best way to duck out of a run was to fake an injury early on so that it would appear legitimate.

Our medical vehicle filled up within twenty minutes, but I kept on running. I was outraged. These tough Marines that America entrusts to protect them can't even outrun a mom pushing her baby? I wanted to unearth every weakling in the unit, so I decided to play a little game of deception. As we approached the end of the Gun Loop, the pack expected that we'd turn off after one complete circuit. I kept going, and we passed the only exit street. About five surrendered. Their wells of fortitude were too shallow.

Unfortunately, these five were higher-ranking Marines; they should have been in better shape. They quit and then grumbled a bit. We went another one hundred feet and stopped. I ordered the formation of fifty Marines to do an about-face, and we all walked by those who had fallen out. They got to walk right past these weak leaders and look them in the eyes. A unit must know their strengths and weaknesses, and there was no hiding anything this time.

I knew that my actions were harsh, but I felt that they were warranted. Weak, out-of-shape Marines, especially officers, put us all in jeopardy. I will always believe that I was doing my duty as a Marine officer and getting my men and women ready for combat while holding up the standards set forth by the Marine Corps. I had never been a by-the-book guy, but this was a crime. My thinking was that, at the very least, they should have been able to run 2.5 miles at the pace of a mother and her stroller—we were Marines, for God's sake!

I did only a couple of other formation runs during my short time as a company commander of this unit. And I didn't play anymore games, but I had made my point. I feel that the incident at least showed those junior Marines what could happen if you let yourself go.

Being home with my family was comforting, but my new job was boring. It wasn't just any boredom but the kind that makes you question whether you're wasting your life away. I went from the high stress of an air controller in a combat zone to fielding a handful of insignificant e-mails and sporadic phone calls. One Sunday, an uptight superior called all officers back into the office to fix the format of a spreadsheet that was "not properly aligned to the left and printed in size 11 courier font." He said it was imperative to have this spreadsheet ready by Monday morning to prepare for Tuesday's weekly meeting. The adjustment took less than five minutes.

Nothing kills the soul more than the combination of a boring unit and bad leaders—they begin to invent things to make people do, just so they can be in charge of the process. To me, this is the best way to convince a

Marine to get the hell out of the Marine Corps at his or her earliest opportunity. It forces you to think existentially. Why are we doing this task? Is this what I did all that training for? I'm supposed to lead. Is this what the Marine Corps is all about?

Marines love deploying on missions. This is what we do best. However, Marines freak out in a garrison office environment. We become lost. Tedious tasks take up the majority of the workday, and meetings become the new focus, the new operations—pointless meetings about pointless subjects. How much longer until the copy machine is fixed? Eighty-nine percent of our Marines completed the online safety training. Next weekend is family fair day, and we need two volunteers for the dunk tank. There is far more to the Marine Corps other than training to fight and war. All the other *stuff* in between is mind-numbing.

Briefing-room rock stars become the kings of the garrison jungle. You may have been excellent in combat. You may have saved lives and accomplished every mission. But here and now, in this briefing room, if you can't make a PowerPoint and deliver it to a drooling audience, then you won't last long. Good luck on getting promoted.

Building and briefing PowerPoint presentations withered my soul. I was dying inside. I developed various anxieties; the simple tasks became incredibly difficult. I became depressed because most tasks seemed meaningless. I was no longer an essential component in the US fighting machine. My world went from loud, busy, and of critical importance to quiet and mostly lame. I was so grateful that my contract in the Marines was ending soon. I was fed up with this lifestyle that was slowly killing my soul.

A close friend, Captain Collins, grappled with the fact that most of the Marines in our unit came to work and had absolutely nothing to do. The mission was absent. How many people are needed to fix a spreadsheet? He described our situation as *precatory*. He explained how he was sickened even more by people pretending to work. He especially became disgusted during periods of complete silence whenever he heard, in the next office over, the tap of a keyboard and the click of a mouse because this was the only labor actually occurring.

"I know that whoever is doing this"—he tapped on the keyboard—"is doing something less important than I am, and I haven't done shit today." He would laugh at how ridiculous this conundrum was.

The environment in our detachment became grim and somewhat lifeless. We simply had nothing to do. I wished that it had been possible to send them all home for months to spend time with their families. I was personally searching for self-worth and needed a goal, something that could pull me out of this rut. I signed up for my first marathon, the San Diego Rock 'n' Roll Marathon.

I became more focused on training for the marathon than on my lame job. I took care of what needed my attention at work and then laced up to hit the gravel roads in the farmlands miles away from town. This desert was a very different scene from Camp Leatherneck and Camp Bastion. No moondust. I never saw a trash fire. This place wasn't Afghanistan; this place was scenic. The sky was permanently blue, and the variable-colored sunrises and sunsets were straight out of an art gallery. We had 360-degree views of a vast and amazing desert. Smells traveled for miles. Eerie echoes resounded seemingly forever. These pure, untouched winds could caress you whenever they wanted.

This desert had almost-reverent sunrises where a supreme being seemed to be looking down on the world from his lofty perch. The caveat was that all this beauty occurred only early in the day or late in the evening. The afternoon temperatures could reach upward of 120 degrees. One of my runs got dangerously hot and gave me a new and highly profound respect for heat. I had always prided myself on being able to thrive in the heat, but I found out that I was indeed a mortal. This place was hotter than running in a garbage bag or sitting in a crappy car with the heat on.

I set out for my twenty-mile run at 6:00 a.m. with a water belt that held a total of six twenty-four-ounce bottles of water, each about three gulps worth. I took off with no hesitation and with my headphones in, headband on, and visor covering my face from the unrelenting sunlight.

My course took me along the Colorado River. The air was so open that I picked up the scent of livestock from three miles away. I caught up to the scent of a couple of ponies roaming aimlessly about in the large backyard of a ranch house. One of the ponies rested his snout on the fence and stared blankly into the yonder. Their view of sand and distant mountains had to get boring, even for a pony. "I know the feeling," I said to myself.

I was on the water's edge of a concrete canal that was twenty feet wide. It was reminiscent of a skater's or snowboarder's half-pipe. I was surprised to see homes built on the bank. I guess this was technically waterfront property, even though it was an aqueduct irrigation canal. The entire theme or motif of Yuma and the Southwest is the man-made structures everywhere. They were the life-support machines to sustain life in this blistering-hot and dry environment. Without them, this would be a dust bowl with very few inhabitants. There was a bit of vegetation along an area where the river would naturally overflow after large snowfalls occurred thousands of miles upriver. Before the advent of air conditioning, only a few thousand people lived in Yuma or Phoenix.

I was now in the midst of these desolate farmlands among millions of heads of lettuce. The sun was merciless; there was nowhere to hide. I ran about ten miles through the farms and then through some quiet neighborhoods. The neighborhoods in Yuma are unique. Residential streets are about twice as wide as the roads in ordinary towns. Houses sometimes have large side yards designed to park a recreational vehicle. Rust-free antique cars sit under tarps or on the side of driveways, well preserved by the arid climate.

I suddenly felt the presence of someone or something closing in on me. I had my headphones in and couldn't hear a thing but sensed its presence. I whipped my head around to see a small, brown, yapping dachshund and a rooster chasing me. For a moment, it felt as if I had been transported into a cartoon. This house had chickens, roosters, and goats roaming the yard. Did Noah's ark crash here?

Once I was free and clear from the pack, it seemed like a good place and time to have some cold, refreshing water that I had frozen the night before. A few gulps of the slushy ice and an energy gel gave me some pep. I imagined myself as Popeye the Sailor Man eating his spinach. Sadly, the cartoon never showed the part where the power of Popeye's spinach eventually wore off to render him weak and flaccid.

I was out of sweat and water after only ninety minutes of running and now found myself in serious survival mode. It was starting to dawn on me that if I didn't get water soon, I would probably fall into a coma and perhaps wake up hours from now with black buzzards feeding on my salty body or, worse, a doctor taking my core temperature with a "silver bullet" (thermometer). I was overheated, and my cramped legs felt like wooden pegs. I skulked my way toward a shady area and then grunted for a half hour. My body sent all the hot blood to my legs. It felt like a steamroller was crushing my thighs and shins. The pressure was excruciating. I began taking breaths as if I were in labor, blowing out with each crushing throb. This sucked.

One question kept running through my head: Why did I run this far?

Now I worried if I could survive the day. In spite of how serious my situation was, I was still so disappointed in my performance and wondering how I would be able to run the upcoming marathon. This run was meant to test my ability to finish a marathon, and I had failed.

Instead of worrying about this stuff, I should have been thinking about how I would get home. I had been resting for over half an hour. My legs were still throbbing, and it was still hotter than hell. Suddenly, a guy appeared from out of nowhere.

"Hey!" he said. "Saw you running past and thought you could use some cold Gatorade." He shoved a bottle of orange Gatorade into my hands, and I drank it down while he watched.

"Are you going to be able to make it back to wherever you came from?" he asked.

I wasn't sure. "I guess. Maybe I'll rest just a few more minutes."

"Well, me and the wife are just sitting around watching TV, if you want to come in and cool off a bit."

"No thanks," I said, out of breath.

My marathon training and upcoming career choices were similar; I didn't know what would happen. Maybe I would collapse halfway through. My wife and I were 90 percent set on getting out of the Marine Corps and weren't prepared; much like the marathon, we were going to wing it. Thoughts of uncertainty rapidly cycled in my mind. How will I make it past mile twenty?

How could I stomach another twelve years in the Marines, putting up with insignificant e-mails and PowerPoints?

I knew this negative projection on the Marine Corps had been conjured up from my depression, but it was my perception nonetheless. One wild card could keep us in the Marines: we considered going to Okinawa because so many other families swore by its beauty and rich environment that bred fantastic experiences. Even with its magnificence, it didn't seem powerful enough to draw us into renewing my contract.

Then, my wife showed me a video of Okinawa. Indigenous drums beat over clips of fire breathers, dragon boats, scuba divers hovering over reefs, and gorgeous beaches. This was a brochure to paradise. Within six months, I would run the marathon. After that, all four of us were on a plane to Okinawa. We said *sayonara* to the United States. We would go on to enjoy three years of a most spectacular life experience, and I would fall in love with running in Asia.

CHAPTER 8

First Marathon

The day before running the Rock 'n' Roll Marathon, I brought my girls to the San Diego Zoo. They loved it. I secretly hated it. To me, zoos are an animal dystopia wrapped underneath a facade of preservation and environmental activism. How is keeping the animals from their natural habitat helping them? Zoos are nothing more than theme parks that earn their revenue from admission, food, and toys. The animals are live displays to inspire children to want rhinoceros-shaped chicken nuggets, cups with a picture of a tiger, stuffed-leopard toys, and colorful snapper toys on those long sticks. Parents and their kids can have fun slurping their zebra icy while riding in a staged safari. I am guilty of being one of these parents who got brain freeze while contributing to this crap.

I had an especially difficult time observing the lions and giraffes because their intrinsic grace was melded into depressed and anxious demeanors. These lions were once noble kings and queens who reigned over their savannahs and watering holes, and now they were stripped of their hierarchical position in the animal kingdom and made into prisoners. They no longer hunted their prey. The zoo fed them prekilled chunks of mystery meat, transforming them into indoor, declawed kitty cats. They were kept inside an exhibit made to look natural with some rocks and a little pond, much like a fish tank with its background picture of some exotic reef.

One lion paced back and forth. Was he plotting on how he would cross the moat and eat one of us for lunch? I saw a couple of bored giraffes lying on the ground chewing something with their legs folded—not what I envision when I think of giraffes. I'm sure they wished they were out in the wild where they could experience the sights, sounds, and smells of a vast desert region alive with hyenas and cheetahs.

Giraffes are stimulated when their long, sensitive tongues wrap around a branch, grass, or leaves. That's their thing. They don't chase, and they don't reign over an animal kingdom. They prance elegantly to a tree and nose around. They are connoisseurs of the vegetation. How would they get their satisfaction in this lot? With their smorgasbord of natural choices having been replaced, they are now fed paltry pellets and chew toys.

This was eerily similar to my military lifestyle. The mundane, worka-day world of my career had transformed me into an indoor kitty. Before the Marine Corps, my stimulation and satisfaction came from the creative en-deavors of filmmaking and writing. Film scripts were replaced with stacks of paperwork—policy letters, investigations, awards, and hundreds of Marine evaluations. This work helped me take care of my family and myself, but my instincts were being gradually dulled the way a butcher's favorite knife is dulled through daily use. Would I forget how to hunt and make a living in the outside world?

Running gave me a way to escape from the zoo for a few short hours each day and explore, think, reflect, smell, and sing at the top of my lungs because no one was around. I wanted to choose for myself which leaves I would chew on.

When our zoo trip ended, I felt the gravitational pull of the upcoming marathon. Step one was picking up the race packet, so I headed to the run-ners' convention and spent the rest of the day there. The place was huge and more crowded than I had expected.

"What does this do?" I asked the sales representative as I sipped my free Sweet Very-Berry smoothie out of my zebra cup.

He pressed the three-foot-long, white rolling-pin object behind his thigh and rolled it down his hamstring and calf as if he were pressing dough. He rolled it up and down while he explained. "Ya see? After a long run, a ton of lactic acid builds up in your muscle tissue and…"

Maybe I blacked out from brain freeze while drinking the icy-cold Sweet Very-Berry because I don't remember the rest. I went there to pick up my race packet and found myself caught in a web of vendors packed into the San Diego convention center. I'm not sure why I bought that guy's large, white rolling pin because now it's just a dusty relic in my attic. Did I really need it? Or did I buy it to fit into the runner subculture?

I'd been running long distance for almost a year, but I never wore running accessories. I actually didn't have much except a Marine Corps green shirt and green long-distance shorts from Afghanistan plus a few clothes from my Goodwill pile in Yuma. How the hell was I supposed to dress? Would they accept me? Who the hell were *they*, anyway? I just didn't want to stand out. I wanted to be one of them.

My entire mind-set was off track and ridiculous. I should have been expending the energy and time in planning my diet, water intake, and running pace. Losing sight of my priorities would catch up and bite me in the ass later. This convention blew my mind. They had accessories for accessories! How does running cost so much money? I naively thought that all you needed was a good pair of shoes to go running. I guess to be a *real runner* you needed these quirky items being pawned off at the runners' convention by smooth-talking auctioneers.

A pair of sunglasses labeled "Runner Sunglasses" flashed an intimidating $200 price tag. A $150 pair of fluorescent shoes glowed from the corner. I became disoriented in the fog of advertising slogans and under the heavy fire of sales pitches. They had a fog machine, for crying out loud.

Their mantras began to ring in my head. Why use a cheap, little iPod Shuffle when you can pay hundreds of dollars for satellite-radio headphones? This got me thinking. My GPS watch is a year outdated, so maybe I should upgrade it. Before I could figure this out, I was accosted with a tall sock sign. Why are these socks thirty dollars? Am I wearing the wrong type? Oh God!

Hundreds of other booths sold miscellaneous running paraphernalia that I never knew existed. I would never have guessed that the running market would be on the same level with golf and fishing. Maybe running has its own aisle at Sports Authority or Dick's Sporting Goods.

When I got back to my hotel room, I sorted through my bag to fish out the only thing I truly needed: my race-number bib. I was officially crazy to hurl myself into a pack of thousands in order to run 26.2 miles. How would I make it? After all, I had run twenty miles only once in the past, and it almost killed me.

After I filled my belly with spaghetti and checked into my room, bedtime came quickly. My wife and daughters stayed in another room to make it more conducive for my much-needed deep sleep. However, I got less than two hours of sleep. That angst eventually churned into adrenaline, and once this potion was in my blood, the Marine in me wouldn't sleep. He was ready for battle.

I showed up early. It was definitely a freak show too—of the wildest kind. Alien creatures had fluorescent shoes peeking from below their tinfoil, silver cloaks. Some wore Superman capes, others sported gorilla costumes, and still others wore sequined Elvis costumes. A team wearing hot-pink tutus chatted calmly as they paced by. Then it clicked: runners have their own unique philosophy on life: "Do whatever the hell makes you feel better when you are running twenty-six-point-two miles."

After that revelation, I loved it. And my love has never faded. From that moment, I would always be in love with the running community. Running became my religion and the source of my identity—spirituality—and now the subculture became my church. Can I hear a heartfelt amen?

I was surprised at how big of a production this marathon was. The area around the starting line looked like a disaster-relief tent city. Pyramids made of bagels and bananas dressed the tables. Masseuses massaged tense shoulders. People of all shapes and sizes stood around doing their breathing exercises and their stretches before the start of the race.

Hundreds of runners were running to support a cause—running for cancer, AIDS, lupus, family members, or national pride. One patriot flew the American flag for the whole race. I am a believer that the first run should be for yourself, just in case you don't finish. I would be shamed if I wore a Marine T-shirt and then quit at mile 15. That would send a negative message to me and everyone else. Nonetheless, the display of so many teams running for a cause bigger than themselves gave me chills. I was teary eyed, but I had some sweat to hide it, of course.

I was in the group expected to run the race in 4:30 (four hours and thirty minutes). I overestimated my ability. I didn't belong there. The boisterous announcer shouted instructions. "First group! On your marks. Get set. Go!"

My group was next. I plugged in only one earbud so I could hear the instructions with the other ear. I was officially off-line and in my own world with my music. "On your marks. Get set..."

I don't remember if he said go, but he didn't need to. The force generated by the mass of one thousand people pulled me forward. Massive crowds lined each side and cheered us on. I'd never experienced such a rousing send-off before. We were all the stars of this event. Hot adrenaline pumped through my body, and I felt euphoric. My feet were weightless butterflies. It felt good to burn up this energy, so I took it a step further and quickly became a junky in need of the next high.

I exploited each open space to zig and zag through any runner who was slower than a 7:30-minute-mile pace. My pace plan, or lack thereof, was to run however fast or slow I felt like running. It seemed to make sense at the time. I ran around people by hopping curbs and running through lawns. I was in a pure manic state. I couldn't get enough of the elation as people cheered us on. Local cheerleader squads rattled their pom-poms; locals came out of their homes with inspiring poster-board signs that read, "You paid for this," "Believe in yourself," and "You are a star."

I felt it was all for me. Happy tears rolled down my salty cheeks as I cruised down mile seven through the Gaslamp Quarter in downtown San Diego. I just knew that I could own this race and finish closer to four hours. My ego was getting gluttonous and on an endorphin binge, guzzling up my energy supply. I felt like Tony Montana in *Scarface* when he stuffs his face into a mound of cocaine and then sits up with the white powder covering his mouth and nose.

The local support was overwhelming. They formed solid corridors along each side, and all had a food treat, a cold drink, or a sign. My mind was already starting to play tricks on me. I had this one ridiculous thought that some of these people were just cleaning out their fridge and donating left-overs to calorie-deprived runners. I never saw a jar of mayonnaise. I took a banana from a man leaning against a shopping cart. In retrospect, he may have been homeless. Did I just steal from a homeless man? For the next mile or so, I prayed the homeless man would be treated to a nice dinner later by one of the cheerleaders.

I got to the halfway point at 1:37, a terrific time for any first-time marathon runner. I still didn't feel like one of them. I was just a runner, not a marathon runner. All those who ducked out at 13.1 miles high-fived and hugged their friends and family. Later, I learned firsthand that most who ran the whole marathon were not as happy when they finally finished the race. The 26.2-mile marathoners hugged their families as if they had just survived a natural disaster, happy to be alive and scarred for life because of their horrific experience.

The "halfers" looked fresh and happy. Their exuberance started me thinking. Maybe I should have quit at 13.1 and been one of those joyful half marathoners who celebrated with loved ones. My legs were still springy, and I had no doubts of finishing strong. I started to think about stopping to have water but wasn't thirsty yet. I seemed to be trucking along just fine.

I sobered up on mile-marker 16 when the devil crept up my upper-thigh area. A mass of runners pulled off to the side at this point to stretch and spray that fancy, numbing anesthetic on their legs. Was this some mandatory stopping point, or did everyone except me know to stop at mile 16? One guy had his leg propped up on a concrete barrier and stretched out straight. I saw him and thought about stopping but was too scared to do it. Besides, I had never stopped on runs before; my well of fortitude had always been deep enough to keep me going.

This marathon was a whole different story, though. My well and my ego finally led to my demise. I ran out of gas and stalled out at mile 17 as my stride turned into a limp hop-jog. My legs felt like waterlogged tree trunks, and my blood turned to sludge. The very top of my right quad felt like a tender piece of meat falling off the bone. My decline was fast and steep. I'd had about eight ounces of water up until this point, so major dehydration exacerbated my poor, depleted condition.

At mile 17.5, I had to make the decision to walk or die of dehydration and stupidity. My body advised my brain. "Hey, pal. I know you have this ego to feed, but your legs are about to quit, if you don't slow down. If you don't give them the proper attention they deserve, you will not finish. You will officially fail. And you may die."

I negotiated with my ego to approve the rationalization: "Although I am walking, I will not consider myself a failure if I still finish." The next three miles were pure torture. I pulled my headphones out so I could devote my concentration to my groin. The runners I'd passed earlier in the race caught up now and zipped past me as if I were a broken-down car on the side of a freeway. My hazards were on, but I was still moving in first gear. The cute, chatty, hot-pink tutu ladies cruised by. The guy with the flag flew past me. Spectators looked on with sympathy and horror. Shouldn't we call an ambulance for this poor fool?

At mile 19, I engineered a type of run-hobble stride that miraculously got me to mile 23. The pain at this point was so severe that it motivated me to go faster so I would finish faster and end the torture sooner. I was pushing through my walls, drilling beyond the depths of my well of fortitude in a desperate search for just-enough toughness to finish. My run-hobble was so slow that the moderate temperature in the seventies brought on hypothermia. My clammy skin was chilled, and my core temp was lowering. I had burned out the flame inside me. Suddenly, I was out of the cold pain zone, and I saw it. There it was just in front of me—the finish line. Finish ahoy! I prayed it was not a mirage.

I started crying; this time, it was obvious because I wasn't sweating. I was once again overwhelmed by the support. Supporters packed in on the left and right of the final one-hundred-yard corridor. We were all-stars once again during this homestretch. I used up the remainder of my body's water on tears. I was going to make it. I looked up at the large timer that read 5:15. The second half was almost four hours.

A lady knighted me with a finisher ribbon and medallion as I crossed the line. I then made my approach to crash-land on the first open space of concrete. I dropped to the ground and went into a giving-birth, labor-like breathing. I was inhaling and exhaling with the frequency of dull throbs shooting through my agonizing legs. I felt stabbing in my groin. My girls, ages three and nine, were there to see their father finish his first marathon. You could see the awe in their faces. They probably had no idea how long this race was, but they could see that I was in pain and struggling to survive every excruciating moment. All of us 26.2-ers were far from the exuberant happiness that the halfers ended with.

I propped my feet up as my girls looked down on me like a team of doctors analyzing my condition on a hospital gurney. After my initial shock, the weight of victory from the finisher medal around my neck at last won out and overpowered the pain.

This marathon taught me some valuable, lifelong running wisdom: Your ego can destroy you. Sometimes, you must leave it behind. Your ego knows no statistics and limitations. Keep it in balance, and it will serve you best. Avoid the urge to indulge in using up all the energy cocktail the crowd supplies in the beginning. Plan what to eat before the race. Figure out the best pace for the run and stick to it.

This was my final challenge while stationed in Yuma, Arizona. My family and I were now off to Okinawa, Japan, where I would peak in my career and face life-changing events that would leave me transformed forever. I would grow all my gray hairs there. I would face more confrontations than I had faced in my entire life so far. I would end up in an emergency room for days with an unexplainable event that would lead to major challenges with my daily running and the termination of my career. I would learn about bad friends and ruthless politics, about family, and about fatherhood. That video brochure of how lovely and exciting it was in Okinawa would deliver on each of the adventures it advertised and way beyond—dragon boats and all. I would also discover and fall in love with Okinawa running.

Up until this point, my roller coaster had no steep thrills or scary loop-the-loops. It was a kiddy ride compared to the journey I was about to take professionally and personally in Okinawa. In some ways, I would begin my tour in Okinawa at a fast and furious pace, much like I had in the San Diego Rock 'n' Roll Marathon. Just like that race, I would return three years later in a hobble-stride similar to the one I'd used crossing that finish line. But, as the saying goes, "The important part of a marathon is not how fast you run it. The only thing that counts is that you cross the finish line."

CHAPTER 9

Oh the Views of Okinawa!

We packed up everything we owned—including our dog, Sarah—and said sayonara to those we loved. We hopped on the *Patriot Express*, the 747 exclusively used by the military to transport service members from Seattle, Washington, to Okinawa (Oki), Japan. Sarah had to fly separate on a commercial airline because they didn't have room for her. I don't recommend flying your dog—ever.

I went to pick her up at Naha Airport in Okinawa the day after we arrived. They wheeled her cage out on a dolly. She was silent. Was she okay? Clipped to the front of her cage was a translucent, green hunk of plastic that was gnawed down to a nub. Forty-eight hours ago, it had been her water bottle. She prefers to eat rugs when she gets major anxiety, but this time she had to settle for whatever was available. She looked scared and dangerous. She was crouched against the back of the kennel, with her head dipped low to the ground—frozen in time and space. She looked up at me like a rabid wolf ready to strike. She seemed disoriented, terrified, and vulnerable from flying in the luggage compartment from Seattle to San Francisco to Tokyo and then to Okinawa.

I called out to her. When she recognized my familiar voice, she yelped. "Arr! Arr! Arr!" She was so happy to see me. I could almost hear her shouting, "My owners didn't abandon me! They do love me!" Her cage was dry, which meant she hadn't peed for two days. I brought her to the nearest field and released her. She peed for at least two minutes and then ran about ten loops around me to burn off all that nervous energy and stress. We had all finally made it to Oki safe and sound. This marked the end of the stressful journey and the beginning of a new chapter in our lives.

My first run in Oki was on the four-mile Habu Trail, inside the perimeter fence of Marine Corps Air Station Futenma. The base is eight hundred feet above sea level, so the top of each hill presents a rewarding panoramic view that looks down on the turquoise East China Sea, with the western coastal towns of Kadena and Chatan as a backdrop. Swells crash on the barrier reefs. The other side of the path is a fluorescent-green jungle that's so dense that you wouldn't be able to see a yellow school bus if it were parked inside it.

As I ran, I'd take in all these new sights, sounds, and smells. Often, I'd think about how so much fighting had been done in the area in World War II. As I ran past the lush jungle, I wondered how anyone had been able to fight here.[27] You can't even walk in this without a machete.

The thick vegetation was alive with loud, intense buzzing that sounded similar to crickets. Day crickets? Eventually, I learned that these were cicadas, insects a bit larger than bumblebees. They would spend the entire day all summer long making this constant buzzing that would annoy anyone. They're curious little critters. Before we knew they were harmless, they terrorized us by flying at our heads and into our cars. That's what they do. They mess with you.

In front of the jungle was a sign with a yellow-spotted cartoon snake that read, "Beware of Deadly Snakes." The venom from a habu bite has the potential to paralyze and kill its prey. Still another sign informed me that running with music was authorized on the trail. A huge plus! This was the first base I'd been to without the stupid policy that bans the use of headphones during physical outdoor activities. At bases where headphones were banned, runners would ordinarily just go off base to run, but they would face busier, more dangerous roads. I was impressed with the Habu Trail's whole package.

---

27 The Battle of Okinawa was the largest amphibious invasion in the Pacific during World War II. Over 80,000 people died.

I was already hyped up about the move. Running here is going to be great. Okinawa will be a fantastic adventure because, regardless of how the Marine thing goes, the running here will be amazing!

Okinawa took tons of adjusting. We had to learn how to drive on the left side of the road. We had to buy cars. I went with a Nissan March, one of the smallest cars on the island. Keep in mind that I am 6 foot 2. Not being able to extend my legs completely would be devastating if my leg cramped. My wife, Kristin, went with the rusty Toyota thing that came equipped with a sliding side door. A decent car cost anywhere between $1,000 and $5,000. I spent $5,000 to buy two cars. Most servicemen and their families drove crappy cars—it made no sense to invest in something you'd leave behind in three years. Also, cars were not a status symbol in Japan—we all had shit boxes to drive.

My family was stuffed into base housing on an old Navy hospital base called Camp Lester. The four of us shared one shower and a tiny sink, the kind you'd see on an airplane. Toothbrushes stood like dominoes on the corner; hit one, and you may knock them all into our tiny toilet. The room was so cramped that you could not shut the door while sitting on the toilet. Yet the breathtaking location made our new, compacted lifestyle all worth it.

A Starbucks was so close that I could hit a baseball over a few homes and into the front window. We were practically on the beach; a four-minute jog would put me on Sunset Beach.[28] The house was ugly but perfect. Our oldest daughter could walk to the school on base.

Once we got all settled in, I would start preparing to take charge of my new detachment. A new form of energy brought on by my future position churned a different flavor of angst within me. I would soon command 107 Marines in a unique, one-of-a-kind detachment that was considered a major strategic national asset by its equipment and highly qualified personnel. Was I—the guy who started out mopping sewage water in the head on board a ship—really going to do this? It seemed surreal at times. Meanwhile, I would venture out on a quest to map more beautiful runs.

---

28 Sunset Beach is a popular tourist destination known for beautiful sunsets. Spectators line up on each clear sunset and take pictures. The beach is close to American Village, which is a trendy, upscale outdoor beach mall.

My next run took me to a place called Taguchi Beach. It looked right out of some coffee-table book filled with exotic paradises on earth.

I found this place on a random run. When I set out on this particular discovery trek, I left my GPS watch in my sock drawer. The roads rumbled with traffic. Oddly, though, there were no horns because honking is illegal here. This would never fly in the United States, I thought as I ran down the side of the road. The cars were tiny. The most common was the Honda Cube. You rarely saw big pickup trucks or any car with a V8. Inside some cars, you could see children moving about freely because there were no child-restraint laws. It seemed strange and really dangerous to this Westerner.

I had no destination planned; I was just out for a run on a journey to a place where I could turn off my apprehension. I ran free and wide open, allowing random thoughts to guide me. *Turn left. Okay. Go this way, no, that way. Okay.* I ran by the Kadena Air Base[29] gate on my right, and to my left was a sparkling, turquoise ocean. I glided onward with this view for a while before hooking toward the water.

The concrete towns were all similar, no matter where you were. Houses were all gray or some form of off-white. Each one had bars on the windows, and I would find out later that they served to protect the windows from frequent typhoons, not crime. There was virtually no crime. The only place I locked my doors was on base.

Young children of about five years old walked by themselves or held hands with another little buddy. They crossed the streets by themselves. Their parents were nowhere around. Okinawan children were allowed to walk independently at an early age. Yes, it was that safe. I couldn't fathom this type of freedom for an American child. Okinawans trusted each other, and I sensed right away that they were way ahead of Americans in this regard. We could learn so much from them.

The town streets were serpentine-like with forks and doglegs. I was soon disoriented and had no clue where I was. The saving grace in getting lost here

---

29 This is a major US Air Force base that holds over twenty thousand airmen and has played a major strategic role since the Korean War.

was that this is an island, and you would eventually get spit out on the beach. My great sense of curiosity got me lost a few times, as I searched for Valhalla.

I finally found a Starbucks with large, concrete *shisa* dog[30] statues guarding the front door. I recall thinking, Wow! Even Starbucks is exotic in this place! I told myself that I'd be sure to hang out there if I could just find it again. The trees were well manicured with wooden braces that mentored their straight, vertical growth and served to hold them up during high winds. Okinawans take pride in their trees and plants. They seem proud of everything.

Store attendants, restaurant workers, lawn crews, and any other worker showed professional respect to all. The ideology this culture shares is to be the best at whatever you do and show respect for humankind. Fast-food restaurants are no exception. At a Popeye's fast-food restaurant, I bought a chicken sandwich with a freshly baked bun and a pickle that was dead center. I imagined an Okinawan fast-food worker carefully placing the pickle on the chicken breast and then bowing to it.

I came out of my run daze and woke up on a beach with a coral cliff covered in palms, shrub spuds, and scattered plants. At the foot was a park with a tall, twisty roller slide. The bottom was made of the same rollers used to push boxes along a track. A canopy above the slide, made of a few bars, protected the little children from flipping out of it. Kids sledded down on cardboard flaps to prevent the fast metal rollers from burning their bottoms. Little, happy kids shot out of the bottom. They made a *U*-turn right away to climb the steps all the way back up to the top.

I found a narrow trail that disappeared into the cliff's vegetation. The entrance was posted with another "Beware of Snakes" sign. Each time I would see these signs, I'd recall a Marine from my same unit who told me a story of how his dog was killed by a habu. He described how the dog's face *melted* before it died. I shivered, thinking about the poor animal's untimely death, but continued on the trail. It led me up to a fifty-foot-high peak. The top cleared away to breathtaking views of the East China Sea. The perch looked

---

30 These dog statues sit on the roofs or at the entrances of most Okinawan businesses or residences. They are meant to keep the good spirits in while protecting from the harmful spirits outside.

out over a river inlet and ocean. Waves crashed into the cliff's side, just like they've done for a million years. A small pavilion with a concrete bench and table stood as the centerpiece, the crown of earth's pearl.

I promised myself that I'd return one day to this beautiful place and do some writing. A steep trail brought me down to a beach that was partitioned within a series of arched sea caves. They formed a series of buttressed, arched doorways. Inside was shaded sand and calm water that gently lapped on the shore. Some bubbles formed, and I could see a couple of scuba divers in black suits with their yellow air tanks bobbing just at the surface. The diving here was supposedly amazing. One day, I asked a master diver where the best spots to dive off the island were. "Anywhere there is water," he said.

The sun was a brilliant amber that was quickly growing darker as it sank into the sea. I followed the coastline back through a town called Sunabe, which is occupied by two types of residents: Okinawans and American divers. The residents are so close to the water that they can walk to it with their flippers on. I ran on top of the three-foot-wide Sunabe seawall. One misstep, and I would fall to the ocean side's jagged coral rocks, where my broken body would then get hammered by the six-foot swells that crashed below. There were also barriers of dolos[31] beneath. A tumble on these, and my head would be nothing more than a pinball bouncing off the protruding knuckles. I would be spared from the crashing waves, but my bludgeoned body would become crab food for sure.

About every fifty yards was a three-foot gap in the wall. I hopped over each gap. Fifteen feet down below, in between the gaps, was a concrete staircase for divers—this would definitely break my back. For some reason, I believed the gain was worth the risk. Instead of being fearful of these dangerous obstacles, I was caught up in the fun of the run, maybe because I was lightheaded and high on life. I was invincible.

The purple-blue ocean was gobbling up the peach sun. I had about twenty minutes of daylight left. The wall, with its treacherous rocks and

---

31 *Dolo* is translated into "knuckle bone" and is a geometrically shaped, twenty-ton object designed like a toy jack. These concrete monsters are grouped together to protect the wall from erosion by the violent storms.

ocean below, invited me to come back anytime. As I stood there, I recalled that first day I went running on the aircraft carrier. I could look over the edge of the deck and view the fierce, unrelenting sea ninety feet below me. It was frightening yet exhilarating.

Today, I leaped with confidence. I had grown sturdy and straight into a headstrong officer. Nothing could harm me. I give most of the credit to my mentors who braced me for life's challenges. The ones I kept in my life took pride in my growth.

CHAPTER 10

To Fly to the Sun without Burning My Wings

The Greek mythical character Icarus flew on wings made of feathers and wax. His father warned him not to get too close to the sun or his wings would melt from the heat, and he would fall to his death. As the tale is told, Icarus ignored his father's guidance, flying very close to the sun, where his wings did indeed melt, causing him to fall to his death. Like Icarus, I flew too high. Luckily, I did not die. My wife pulled me out just in time before my wings melted.

Red streetlights swung back and forth, causing an odd reflection on the black, wet streets. On Monday, January 11, 2012, the town of Chatan slept as I flew high at 3:00 a.m. My shirt was off, and my pants were wet. I had no shoes. I was running back from an early morning swim with our dog, Sarah. I stopped in front of a puddle and stared down at the shape of the full moon reflected on the water's surface. Sarah took a drink and wrinkled the moon. I crept down with her, and we breathed in the still-cool air.

My heart was beating out of my chest. I was extremely hyper to the point that it made me dizzy and delusional. Within a few hours, I was in the emergency room. I had slept for a total of about ten hours during the past month. The months before that hadn't offered many more.

"The shot or the pill?" the doctor asked. There were no more options. It was late, and the doctors had to go home. Their attempts to bring me down had failed. They had tried bringing in my wife. They had tried calling my mother and father back home. I had been at the hospital since 7:00 a.m., and it was now 11:00 p.m. The doctors at Camp Lester Naval Hospital were way beyond the end of their shift. They wanted me to eat something. They also wanted me to go to sleep, but I wasn't listening to anything they told me or offered.

I was in nirvana and didn't want them to take it away. I was in a manic state; my thoughts were all over the place: "They're the bad guys. They just want to take me down because they don't have my power. They're not enlightened. They're asleep like everyone else. Their brains are polluted with toxins like sugar and alcohol that rot the brain. The food they want me to eat is poison because they want to take me down."

I was flying high and thinking on a level beyond their understanding. I was delirious. More crazy thoughts came as the doctor prepared to medicate me. I was thinking, "They just want to bring me back down to their world of the slow-minded zombies. They want to kill the magic inside me."

My dad called from back home. He interrupted these wild thoughts. "You have to take what they are giving you, Chris. You have to listen to them. This has gone too far now. Take what they are trying to give you." He pleaded with me over the phone, but I was sure he was one of them. He's talking in code. He doesn't really want me to take it. I still refused, but they gave it to me anyway.

The doctor interrupted again. "You're getting one of these." He held up a needle. "It's not your choice anymore." Fade to black.

The shot knocked me out. I woke up periodically in my long slumber to a lady monitoring me from a chair nearby. She never took her eyes off me, and she scribbled something on her clipboard each time I opened my eyes. While I slept, Navy doctors told my wife that I might be flown to a more advanced facility in San Diego for six months. From there, I would be separated from the Marine Corps.

One health administrator handed Kristin a pamphlet titled, *How to Cope with Losing a Loved One.* "He may never see reality again. There is a chance that Chris will be in this state for the rest of his life," one doctor said to her.

Kristin was shaken up, to say the least, not knowing if I would snap out of it. She was so worried about our family that she began investigating the ways to get our belongings from storage back to the United States. In her mind, the military was going to toss her and my children out on the streets.

I woke up thirty hours later. It was morning. I was dizzy. A nurse escorted me to the bathroom and watched my every move. She handed me the face razor and then stared at me as if I would try to use it as a weapon at any moment.

"Are you thinking of hurting yourself?" she asked me very slowly as if I were a crotchety, old man.

I assured her I was not. "I love life too much to harm myself or others."

I was stripped of my rank and reduced to a hospital robe and brown socks with little white grips on the bottom.

After morning hygiene, I had an interview/evaluation with a panel of the hospital's specialists. The panel rattled off their invasive and intimidating questions. I felt as if the world was against me. I was in their petri dish, under their microscopes. I was scared of what they may do. I thought they were going to shove electric paddles in my mouth and shock me.

I thought I'd just play it cool and get the hell out of here. They're trying to erase all my creativity. They want to kill my mind! All the while, I kept repeating myself to them. "I'm fine. I'm okay. I just didn't have much sleep." They seemed more intrigued than concerned. It felt like a criminal and they were the police interrogating me under bright lights until I would finally break. Would they send me to a loony bin?

Thirty-six hours earlier, I had been admitted to the emergency room with extreme sleep deprivation and a heart rate around ninety beats per minute (twice my normal forty-five). I had felt hyper for a couple of months before this event but never knew the implications of sleep deprivation. Missing sleep gave me more energy, enough that I ascended to a higher plane as if I were Icarus and to another world filled with creativity and glorious optimism.

"I can do anything and everything," I would secretly tell myself. My creative aperture opened up like a dilated pupil in a pitch-black room. I began to write,[32] draw, paint, sing to myself in the car, play the guitar, drive random

---

32 This is when I began writing this book and five others. Most of my projects today were started during this episode.

routes, touch things just to feel their texture, and smell anything natural. I ran in lightning storms. I was a sensory vacuum cleaner, sucking up all information available because it was the fuel for my creative fire. I felt 100 percent in tune with nature, but I was 100 percent in need of major attention. My entire right brain lit up like a Christmas tree, and I was in nirvana. One specialist later told me that my frontal lobe completely disconnected, leaving me in this happy state. Then, when I finally got too close to the sun, my wife shut it all down by calling a friend to take me into the emergency room. She was fed up with my bizarre, hyperactive moods.

In the emergency room, I was loopy and funny and wouldn't stop screaming to people about my new insights into the world. "War! We're going to war!" I said because I saw a large letter *W* on the wall. I had flown a long way from reality. They scanned me for encephalitis, tested me for drugs, and took brain scans. You could see all the doctors and nurses thinking, "What is wrong with this guy?"

My commanding officer had tremendous power over Navy doctors and used it. Commanding officers can use the influence of the Marine Corps and the career of the Marine. The Marines desperately needed me to command the detachment, because I was the only captain available with qualifications to do the job. To bring me back on the team, they needed me to cooperate.

One of my superior officers, the executive officer of my squadron, came to the hospital and lambasted me. "You aren't getting it, Captain Bolender! You aren't listening to the doctors or your wife! You may lose your children and your career unless you listen. You are in control, Captain!" His scolding was borderline abusive. I felt as if I had to vomit, and I swore I was going to have a heart attack.

I was dizzy. I was confused. I had to lie down to make the room stop spinning. After the executive officer made each of his points, I nodded like a child who just realized he'd been bad. I envisioned a father figure standing over me, pointing his finger and saying, "Now, son. You know that's not right. Do you know what you did wrong?" Nod. I was being submissive, but I still didn't really know what I'd done wrong. I knew that I wasn't doing something right. He was in charge, right? I had to shut up and get better. What the hell was wrong with me?

One day, while in the hospital, I met a bald guy in a red sweater out in the hallway. He was in for posttraumatic stress disorder. He gave me some good advice. "Bro, don't say anything. Just play it cool. Just keep your eyes low and answer their questions. Just do this, and you'll make it out in no time. Be smug."

I took his advice, and he turned out to be right. He'd been in the hospital a few times and knew the system. I kept quiet. After tons of sleep, I came to and was discharged from the hospital. I just shut up, and they let me go. Three days after that, I went for a follow-up.

The doctor in charge of my case gave me some advice, "Stay away from the hospital for ninety days, and you'll get a clean bill of health. No deploying off the island until this time is up. Do your job, and don't freak out again. Get eight hours of sleep every single night. Follow these instructions, and you'll be able to pursue your next position as a detachment commander."

I took the deal. I knew that I could lose it all if I didn't listen to their advice. I had a newfound respect for the impact of stress and lack of sleep. I was badly injured and, from this point on, needed to ensure good sleep.

Kristin and I had a conversation over lunch a few days later about what had happened. "That bald guy in there is the one who helped me get out of that place," I told her while eating my sandwich.

She looked at me as if I were crazy again. "There was no bald guy on that ward, Chris," she said slowly. There was an uncomfortable silence—the kind that occurs when something extremely significant was said.

I wasn't sure what to say. Was I still crazy? Was I really *completely insane*? Now I was seeing people who didn't exist. In the space of a moment's time, I decided to play it off, still afraid that they would lock me away and give me shock therapy. "Oh?" I finally said. "Maybe he wasn't bald."

She put down her fork and cocked her head. "Wait, you mean the guy wearing the red sweater? Yeah, I guess he was bald." I was relieved that I at least wasn't hallucinating.

About four months later, Kristin and I began to try to investigate what happened and why. I hadn't even been told my diagnosis. I was told only to stay away from the hospital.

I looked back at the past year of my life for answers and began the healing process with Navy doctors. We learned that I had to balance lots of things in my life in order to keep myself healthy. I didn't want to have a heart attack. The key was to monitor and balance my energy levels in everything I did. I had to trim down my late-night work and projects.

My first step was to run more, but I wanted to make sure it was okay. "Is there anything wrong with running once a day?" I asked the doctor.

He smiled. "Yes. With your energy levels, you should probably run *twice* a day."

Running and some additional sleep medications stabilized my energy levels and drastically improved my quality of life. I had the best team of doctors, but this one in particular may have saved my life. She put me on track and taught me how to deal with insomnia and sleep deprivation. She kept me healthy and helped me maintain my position as a captain in the US Marine Corps and as a detachment commander. She taught me that my ambition was a gift, but my energy would go out of whack unless it was kept in check.

I now had to abide by a daily routine for the rest of my life. Running became a form of energy dialysis for my brain and a necessary apparatus for my survival. I rely on my legs for a healthy brain.

CHAPTER 11

Thailand Sewage

I had been out of the hospital for only a few months and was scheduled to take over the detachment in a few days. It was going to be tough because the gentleman captain, whom I was replacing, was untrustworthy and out to get me. He had a crooked smile, which is body language for a form of inauthenticity.

Out of professional respect, I will refer to the captain who led this tribe as "Captain Cliff." For some reason, he wanted to vilify me and contaminate my reputation by spreading caustic rumors to subordinates and superiors alike. He was trying to erode my foundation and trap me underneath a short ceiling. I found out on our first day in Thailand that he asked my future junior Marines if they "felt concerned about my inability to lead," thus injecting doubt among the general population.

I believe this was a reaction to my refusal to participate in adulterous acts out in town with the crowd. Things such as prostitution, staying out past curfew, and partying until a couple of hours before the following day's operation were common with him. I was on my own island. This was a sociological case of weak people conforming to illogical seats of power, sanctioning an evil hegemony. A bad military leader will trickle his amorality and weak fortitude down to the lowest ranks and rot the entire team from the inside out.

The trouble was that no one saw his bad leadership except me. My perception of him was clearest because I had never developed a relationship with him. I owed him nothing. My role here was to hold the moral ground and do what was best for the unit. I had to live in a state of quarantine.

"Lead by example" and *ductus exemplo* (Latin for "lead from the front") are the two fundamental mantras of all Marine officers. In this case, he was leading by *bad* example, and because he was leading from the front, he was pulling the whole unit down with him. Blasphemy to the institution! The unit was infected; they were overrun with filth, like a murky, green pool filled with algae and bubbling over with a foul odor.

I vowed to be the chlorine that would shock the muck out of the system and turn the green water clear. Bucking the trend and doing what is right can sometimes win you a lonely life. I had no friends, and soon I would be in some serious confrontations to capture the flag.

Nothing drains my emotions more than a heated confrontation—no matter the outcome. Our three weeks in Thailand would start off chain reactions of confrontations over the next two years. I had no idea how rotten these people really were and no idea what I was getting myself into. Only my wife and I will truly ever appreciate how difficult this time was. I've heard from hundreds of steadfast leaders that if you're doing your job the right way as a commander, you're a lonely soul.

The source of the muck, Captain Cliff, fired the first shot at me. It was an ambush. I was walking around our operation site when he jogged up to me. He sported a stoic and slightly crooked grin. "Your wife called and said that something bad happened and you need to call her right away."

"Crap! What happened, Cliff?"

"I'm not sure. That's all I know."

I panicked. My mind went into hypercreative mode and began to imagine tragic scenarios. My dad crashed his plane into a mountain? My brother had a heart attack? My mother, whose mother died in her sixties, followed suit? A UPS truck hit my sister? One of my daughters? My mind raced through all these possibilities as I sprinted to headquarters.

I flung the door open to the commanding officer's office. His staff looked startled by my abrupt and somewhat brash entrance. I shouted. "Sir, I need to use the phone immediately. I have a family emergency."

I finally got a hold of my wife via Skype. "What happened?" I asked, panting.

"I didn't want to tell you yet because it's kind of embarrassing," she said with an expression that was a hybrid sad face with a smile. This was the face she decided to make to tell me that the bird had died.

This may have been funny to Captain Cliff, but this was actually tragic news. I loved that bird. We went through a life-changing transformation together. This lovebird had caught my eye in the pet shop when he twisted his neck to look at me as soon as I turned down the aisle. I strolled by, thinking how it was a bit strange. Was this bird that intuitive? I circled the aisle again, and when I rounded the corner, he cocked his head to the side at me again with his orange face and beautiful green feathers. Kristin tried it, and he did the same thing.

We had to get him, and we named him Uncle Bill (after my uncle who loved birds). When we brought him home, he was so timid that he wouldn't step out of his cage. When he finally did, he couldn't fly. He would flap his wings like a frustrated turkey, unable to launch like most avian species. After I let him out dozens of times, he began to trust me, and I could get him to stand on my finger. Soon after this, he began flight training. I would swing my hand into the air to give him a boost. In a few days, he could flutter-leap from my finger to another object a few feet away. After a few more days, he could fly to the top of the bookshelf.

A few days after that, his flying was perfect. He was able to zip up thirty feet into a tree. The awesome part was that he would come back. He would swoop right back down to my shoulder, on top of my head, or on top of the dog. On top of the dog! During this same time, he taught me confidence in my intuition and creativity. After all, if I could teach a bird how to do something extraordinary, then I could do other awesome things. He was my companion during my manic episode. I taught him to fly, and then I began to fly myself, but I had trouble coming down.

The other part that sucked about this whole ordeal was the fact that Captain Cliff knew the bad news. He lied by telling me he had no further information. He thought a dead bird was so insignificant that it would be okay to play the trick. He did not respect me. Before the prank, he told the commanding officer's staff how I would soon run in their office, panicking. He got everyone in on the joke. The worst part is that he led me to believe that someone in my family may have actually died. He was okay with watching me enter a state of frenzy.

This was the last straw. I was going to get his ass out of the way and take charge of this monkey circus. I saw right through his childish games and decided to get serious.

I got out my figurative scalpel. I showed up early, 5:00 a.m., on my first day as detachment commander. I wanted to be ahead of everyone else and catch them off guard. I began to cut out the cancer in my detachment. I asked Captain Cliff to stay off *my* site. I went after the lieutenants first because I saw them as the most impressionable, and their demise would threaten the integrity of the unit. Officers lead from the front. Two had the cancer. I took the first one out with one well-aimed shot.

The junior second lieutenant had been partying with *Cancer* Cliff all night until he ended up face down in a sewage ditch, left for dead. When he showed up the next day, he was supposed to be manning a console, watching for any air-control safety concerns. He was a danger to our mission and the life of every pilot under our control. When I walked in the tent, his face was buried into his arms, and he was out cold. He reeked of alcohol.

It was unacceptable, a crime. To lead by example, I had to quarantine him. I berated him. "If you ever show up drunk to work ever again, I will charge you. Now get the hell out of my face!"

The next contestant was supposed to be my right-hand man. He was my executive officer, second in command of my detachment, and he was not enforcing the onsite uniform policy I had enacted. *He* wasn't even following it.

"Can I see you for a second?" The way I said this was hardly a question. We got into the tent, and I yanked the zipper down, closed. I chewed his ass at the top of my lungs, lighting him up with my lexicon of expletives. He looked stunned and was completely speechless.

His reply was short. "Yes, sir."

Within twenty-four hours, I honed in on number three, one of my highly qualified instructors. I had my eye on this Marine for being too close to the junior Marines and appearing to be a weak leader and part of the Cancer Cliff Alliance. That evening, he was thirty minutes late for his watch. I threw questions at him: "You like to show up late? What do you mistake me for, some pushover? What example are you setting by waltzing in here late?" Obviously, we both knew the answers.

His reply was also short. "Yes, sir." I found out later that this was his birthday. Well, happy birthday.

I became stressed out and isolated. I was also getting threats from the commanding officer that he would fire me if I failed. I still wonder what Captain Cancer Cliff told him. I did a good job hiding it, but I became emotionally whipped from all the confrontations. I needed to recharge on a run.

I went out for a relaxing jaunt through the Royal Thai Air Force enlisted housing. They were mostly beat-up, low-cost homes. The enlisted men lived in poverty. Most of the men in this neighborhood worked second jobs. We would call for a taxi and get picked up by a Thai airman whom we had just worked with earlier, controlling aircraft.

"Hello," a group of folks said from their tin-roofed porch that was tucked between a few scrapped cars.

I passed them and waved back. The blood-orange setting sun maintained high temperatures and lit up the heavy, white smog that smelled like burnt tires. A stench rose with the late-afternoon steam. Next to the road were ditches filled with water. These ravines had been dry on my first couple of runs. We had about five hundred Marines on this base, and after a couple of weeks, these ditches turned into canals. The high tide of American sewage wastewater spilled into yards. These poor enlisted men, tucked away at the back of the base, had to smell our excrement and walk in it every day. And they still waved hello! Then, the stench drifted, and a delicious scent of Thai food filled the air. They may be dirt poor, but they're eating well, I thought. Heck, they're even happier than a majority of Americans I've crossed paths with.

I was finishing up my three-mile run with a good old-fashioned sprint the last couple hundred yards. I finished running on the nice side of the base, which was in an upper-class neighborhood. This was the officers' base-housing section.

Because I was a sweat-soaked Marine walking in the middle of the street in this scorching heat, I got the attention of a wife in one of the gorgeous homes. "Are you crazy?" she asked.

"Well, yes. I technically am," I answered, grinning.

"Would you like a cold drink of water?" she asked. "You could come inside and cool off, if you like."

"No thanks, but thank you for letting us stay here on your base and in your country." She laughed at my comment.

From behind me, I heard a deep male voice. "Hey, Marine," he said.

I walked toward this older man, figuring he was much higher ranked. With a stern face, he asked me a question. "Do you know that lady?"

I nodded.

"Man, what you said to her was worth its weight in gold."

It had been a long time since someone recognized me for doing something positive. It seemed like no one liked me and everyone was against me—at least *he* was a fan.

My comment of thanking the lady for letting us stay here had impressed him so much that he presented me with his lieutenant colonel reward coin. In the military, commanders hand out these coins to troops to show appreciation or award them for a job well done. As an officer, rewards are few and far between. I appreciated the gesture.

He handed me the coin. "That's what being a Marine is all about."

This little bit of encouragement, combined with the run, was enough to keep me in the ring in my fight to take charge of the detachment.

Later on, it was confirmed that I was officially at war with Captain Cliff when I was sitting at the base bar. He showed up with all the senior detachment leadership. I greeted him with a hello nod, and his gang walked right past me and sat at a nearby table—no hello, no acknowledgment. Sometimes, doing the right thing means that you will have to be the outsider. I felt as if they were the cool kids in a high school cafeteria, and I was the nerd whom no one wanted to sit with. This immature treatment is uncommon among Marine Corps officers—tact is our bread and butter. They had no idea how strong I was. I would win this fight.

Two months after I took command of this detachment, Captain Cliff was charged with a form of domestic violence. This story went all around the base, like the stench from one of those garbage fires. His empire crumbled overnight.

Allegedly, one night, a man and his family showed up at Captain Cliff's house to look at his minivan for sale. They approached the door to the house and heard screaming. The man entered the residence, and Captain Cliff had a knife up to his wife's neck. His five children were watching. Years later, he was charged and kicked out of the Marines on other-than-honorable conditions. He was suffering from some of his own demons and should have never been in charge of Marines. His wife is a sweet lady and never deserved what she got. Unfortunately, he killed himself in 2015.

The lieutenant who had showed up drunk went on to become my best lieutenant and very successful, taking a detachment of his own.[33] Over the years, we became friends. To this day, he says that the confrontation when I threatened his career was life changing. I'm glad I trusted my gut. You can never go wrong when you take the higher ground.

---

33 Three of my lieutenants became detachment commanders.

CHAPTER 12

"Ductus Exeplo" (Lead from the Front):

The Time I was a Lonely Detachment

Commander Leading 107 Marines

After six months, I became the new detachment commander of the Tactical Air Operations Center, Marine Air Control Squadron-1. I took command of Marines and well over $100 million of air-defense and air-control equipment that was deemed a limited national asset. We were also considered forward deployed, and our mission was to be trained and ready to deploy on a moment's notice anywhere in the Pacific. The general of First Marine Aircraft Wing preached three words to his eight thousand personnel: "Readiness, readiness, readiness."

Once we got back to Camp Futenma, Okinawa, I took my troops on a formation run on the Habu Trail. This was more difficult than the Arizona flat track on the Gun Loop that I took my last detachment on. And because these Marines were of the same breed as my last unit, they were physically soft.

By the end of the pathetically slow run, I lost half the detachment. After the physical gut check, I made it clear to these men and women that I would hold them responsible to abide by the physical standards and expectations of the Marine Corps. I didn't make many friends this day. I made a commitment to my commanding officer and these Marines that I would get every one of the 107 ready for war.

Two months before I took command, on November 17, 2011, President Obama had declared the Pacific as the number-one priority of our military. He was informing the American public of this shift in priorities. For service members, he was ordering them to be prepared. To accomplish this task, I would have to do some deep cleaning within this unit. A mentor of mine, a much-higher-ranking gentleman, told me that I was taking charge of a unit that reminded him of a psychedelic scene in the film *Apocalypse Now*. This scene takes place during the Vietnam War. Christmas lights are strung in the tents, and troops smoke marijuana and trip on acid in an anarchy void of discipline filled with light trails and debauchery. This was the precedent my mentor had set.

During my first interview with my boss, the commanding officer of our squadron[34] counseled me. "My advice to you, Captain Bolender, is not to go into this unit and move everything that is on the right side to the left side on your first day. Sit back and observe for a few months, and then enact your changes." I accepted his advice graciously, as I had no choice in the matter. It was too late to follow it, however.

What he did not know is that, on my first day, I technically already had literally moved every piece of furniture from the right side of our building to the left side. I didn't have time to sit back. The detachment didn't seem to want to accept me at first. During the first few weeks, I made some major adjustments and adjusted some bad attitudes. Not only were they out of shape, but the leaders were unprofessional. The blind were leading the blind. Marines showed up to work in workout clothes. Junior Marines smoked in the front of the building (not okay on a base). The place looked like a dump.

I generated a list of things that would change and called a meeting. Their faces were surprised, and the infected ones looked devastated. This was a

---

34 The hierarchy of units started with a detachment, up to a squadron, and then up to the air wing. Squadrons have multiple detachments, and air wings have multiple squadrons.

new era. No matter what, the direction of this detachment would be corrected. As a sergeant major[35] once said, "A unit of Marines is just like an airplane. They are never technically level. They are always either going up or down."

The cleaning phase drained my soul. I didn't trust a single officer or senior-enlisted Marine in my unit. During this challenging time, I relied heavily on the love and support from my wife and some advice from my father. I believe true leaders in the military have few friends and lead lonely lives in the workplace. Sometimes, you have to be the bad guy. Sometimes, a unit is sick or infected, and groups of people become rotten and need to be fixed. I had to stay balanced and follow through with my promise.

I would escape on runs to rid myself of the emotional poison. I began forming a friendship with running, much like I would with a person. After all, it was always there for me, and it took care of me whenever I needed it.

I was beaten down after a few months and needed some change—a glitch to mix things up. It was all work and no play for me. Thank God my mother-in-law came to visit. I'd been slaving away at work and was burned out. For the past month or two, I hadn't done much writing, and runs were keeping my emotional pulse alive. I had no friends. My wife and I had been falling victim to life's 7:00 a.m. to 5:00 p.m. work grind. Like the habu's venom, my job was causing a paralysis to my soul.

We took my mother-in-law to the city of Nago (Japanese word for "North") to the Okinawa Aquarium. At the "water zoo," we could sip on icy drinks and watch the largest whale shark in captivity twirl in his tank like a beta fish in a champagne glass. I'm sure the intelligent animal was depressed. Such creatures are not free to explore the world; they're not fulfilling their purpose on earth and in the food chain. They're reduced to performing tricks in order to sell children stuffed animals and lunch pails. Was this my life too?

I was happy to get away with the family and show off Okinawa to my mother-in-law. These types of minivacations were sparse because of my Marine responsibilities. I was trying my best to relax and enjoy our trip, but I was stuck in Marine mode and was all wound up inside because of the various pressures.

---

35 A sergeant major is an E-9, the highest enlisted rank in the Marine corps.

With great power comes great responsibility. Here I was in this beautiful place, but I had a storm inside. I was light-years away from enjoying life.

Our hotel was just a few blocks south of the aquarium and across the street from the water. The morning after our trip to the water zoo, I awoke to the sun reaching through the airy, white window curtains. My back was a bit sore from my night's sleep on the tatami mat. The morning light refracted off the beige bamboo floors.

I drew the curtains. The window framed a series of small felt-covered mountains in the distance. The coastal highway curved with the edge of the island, leaping over three bays. The last of three bridges ended on the eastern island of Anno.

My mother-in-law also scoped out this fine Sunday morning and the deep-turquoise sea. "I might go for a run," I said to her.

"How far do you think those bridges are?" she asked.

"What's that, about two miles to the end of the road?" I asked, turning to face her.

"I think you're right on the mark. I bet that is exactly two miles each way." She seemed fairly certain.

I inserted my soft iPod earbuds and started my glide along the Nago coastal highway. The sun hadn't quite matured and was still masked by the green, felt ridge and a canopy of trees, weeds, and roses that arched over the sidewalk where I started this little run. I ran smack into a spider web. "Why doesn't the web ever hit my neck? Always the face!" I thought while pulling the sticky lines away from my face. That poor little spider must have been spinning his food trap all week, and here comes this clumsy, 6-foot-2 human.

I was running in rhythm with my favorite music. I was in my sanctuary, my world protected from the boiling stress. I stole any view of the water I could through the canopies. Something about that water always calms me when I see or hear it. I've always had a natural gravitational pull toward it. This was going to be a great run.

A lady just popped out of nowhere like a jack-in-the-box—surprise! She was squatted down so low and concealed by a bush that I couldn't see her until it was almost too late. Good thing I didn't mow her down. I juked and missed her. I turned around, and she looked at me with a frightened, deer-in-the-headlights expression. She looked extremely puzzled, probably wondering where I'd come from and why an American was in this remote part of Okinawa. Immediately, I wondered if she hated me. I ran on as she continued staring after me in confusion. For the next mile, I wondered what the Okinawans really thought of Americans. Did they all think we were occupiers? This had been American soil until 1972, when we turned it back over to the Japanese, but we never left, still occupying a significant portion of Okinawa.

I hung a right turn toward one of the bridges that I had seen from my hotel balcony. The water was just ahead. I could see the bay that rests just past the seawall. The seawalls in Japan are pieces of art. Graffiti is legal here, and the Okinawans embrace it. Each section has an extravagant mural on it.

The first one I saw showed this particular view of the bay, much as I saw it in that moment. "Maybe someone wanted to immortalize the beautiful view," I thought as I ran past it. The next seawall depicted two Japanese girls smiling and holding up a ring between them that resembled a Hula-Hoop. Inside the ring was a lively scene with all the elements of the sea: dolphins jumping out above the waves, wind swirls on all sides, and a bright sun behind them. The artist had captured a happy moment that would last until the sun, winds, and time would finally erase them.

A hot morning sun was making its debut finally. I ran along the seawall for about a half mile until I was out of land on the first bridge. My stride was still springy, and my mood was elevated. I got to the big, white bridge that stretched across to tiny Sesoko Island. Right before it, I stared down at the tiny beach with little waves splashing on the calm sand. Not a footprint polluted it. I spent a few seconds thinking about ways to get down to the beach and get in that nice, cool water.

On both sides of the bridge, the calm, turquoise ocean was amazing and just as lovely as it had been from the hotel balcony. I was inside the frame now, as if I had jumped into a large, colorful painting. The bay was remarkable and glassy, calm enough to barefoot ski. It would be a great day to take a nap in a canoe that rocked slightly with the tide or on a sailboat anchored in the bay. As the boat would rock back and forth and the anchor line would stretch and creak, I would take long breaths of fresh, salty air.

The wind, the deep-turquoise water, the little island beyond the bridge, and the sunlight on my back all worked together to alleviate my stress. I ran. My stress leaked out. I was on top again. Yes! Innately, I knew that this was why I ran. I glanced down at my watch to see how long it had taken me to get to nirvana—approximately thirty-four minutes. I smiled and pushed harder until I crested the top of the bridge and then relaxed and let my hips unravel as I sped downward. This was a helpful trick taught to me years earlier by that sergeant in Officer Candidates School while running down a hill on the brutal endurance-test run. "Relax your hips and cruise, candidate."

Looking at the water through the cracks on the steel part of the draw-bridge was like looking through a fan. This brought to mind childhood memories of walking on piers in Florida and looking down at the surfers un-derneath. This was one of many relaxing memories that started to flow.

I was headed back now with about four miles under my belt. I felt lighter, like I do sometimes when I leave church. Instead of my sins being gone, I was forgiven of all stress—all of it poured out with the buckets of sweat that my body cried. I was suddenly at that spot where I could quickly move from feel-ing ecstatic to feeling like passing out.

My shirt was completely wet. I was dripping about a gallon an hour, and soon I'd be out of water and out of gas. I imagined the people rushing to my aid. I had no identification. And it would ruin my family's entire weekend. We had plans to go off to the Okuma Okinawa resort later in the day, and I wanted to be on that beach.

These thoughts occupied my brain the rest of the way. I entered my time-warp runner's zone, and abracadabra—poof!—I was at the hotel room, where I made myself a cold bath. I closed my eyes and finally relaxed, welcom-ing those images, so fresh in my mind, of running in that beautiful picture with turquoise water, felt mountains, and untouched sand. As I sank into the cold bathwater, all the noise and chaos of the world went quiet. What a run!

CHAPTER 13

The Lights in South Korea

Cold wind lashed at the tip of my nose. My nostrils were frozen stiff and could not hold back the liquid. A cold drop remained beveled on the point of my nose, as if I were a toddler with the sniffles. My cheeks burned with each icy breeze. I pulled the shirt over my hands to trap my body heat. Around me were snow, ice, and a gray sky. My strides crunched the snow. The hairs stood up on the back of my neck because this place creeped me out. South Korea was a strange land, and I never really enjoyed my time there. But when the general calls and tells you to go, you go.

Just beyond the barbed-wire fence was a farmer. She wore a head scarf and was bundled in layers of rags and winter drab. She looked like a babushka. One of her hands reached out from the bundle and tugged at the dark-gray detritus soil. "What the heck is she reaching for in that cold dirt?" I wondered. This was all barren land as far as I could see. She moved in a torturous motion, as if her blood had turned to sludge. South Korea didn't make sense to me.

BOOM! BOOM! Two gunshots rattled the wax in my ears. Shooting? Really? A flock of grumpy birds scattered toward the clouds. Were the guards shooting someone? This was one of several South Korean riddles.

A truck zoomed past me. "Wait a minute. It's a Wednesday, and this is the only truck or vehicle that has passed me in the past two miles," I thought. This place was abandoned. I didn't see anybody. It seemed artificial, staged, and made up to look like a fake South Korean military base. I saw tons of buildings but no movement. I saw empty playgrounds overtaken by weeds crawling through piles of snow. Maybe the people had downsized their military.

The rotted playground was similar to the one I saw on a base in Thailand. These playgrounds became a theme on American allied bases. I imagined a scenario where the US government installed them in the post–World War II era when we pushed our American imperialism on the world—a public-relations campaign to glorify capitalism over communism. Unfortunately, the American slides and monkey bars never caught on. Perhaps the Koreans didn't want to be rude and take the equipment down, so they just kept it up. This way, when America asks, "How is that playground we got you?" they can appear to be appreciative. "It's still out front. Thank you."

A group of South Korean Soldiers marched toward me. South Koreans are conscripted, not voluntary. All must serve two years, so there are many of them. They also have no ethnic diversity, so they all look very similar. Most of them wore thick, black-framed Woody Allen/San Francisco–entrepreneur eyeglasses. As I jogged by them, I was surprised that they did not greet me. I was a guest on their base, but they didn't care. This would become a common practice each time I was deployed to a South Korean base. We have protected them for over fifty years, and they didn't even say hello or give professional courtesies. I was not impressed. I was there helping them and didn't get so much as a nod.

Knee-high snowbanks lined each side of the road. A flatbed truck pulled up, and a dozen South Korean Soldiers jumped out with shovels. They shoveled the dark South Korean dirt onto a patch of ice on the road. I guess they don't use salt to melt ice on the roads. I have no idea if it works. I ran by the chain gang and felt like a ghost. Not one Soldier looked at me or acknowledged my presence. Were they Korean robots? Was this a big play to give me the illusion that this base is actually occupied? I imagined a man who was a director in charge of keeping this base looking like a real operation. I imagined what he said to this team a few minutes ago. "This Marine just passed our abandoned school and playground, so we need to dispatch the 'bots to keep him thinking this is all legit. One more thing: fire a couple of more shots in the air."

I went to South Korea a total of six times in three years, and each time I thought the place was ugly. The Soldiers never seemed to see or acknowledge me at all. Was I a ghost? Gray buildings, ice, abandoned playgrounds, and everything they did was weird, and weird things sort of freak me out.

Half my trips there were high-stress situations. I would leave on a moment's notice after ordered on a phone call that would go like this: "Captain Bolender, pack your bags. We need your Marines to [blah, blah, blah] so be ready to get on the bird in twelve hours. Can you do this?"

I told him the same thing each time. "Yes, sir." I would say it with confidence, but later I would wonder. Why did they trust me? How could they? I was just recently the sleep-deprived crazy guy in the hospital, and now I'm in charge?

Kristin did not enjoy my telling her I was leaving so quickly. She didn't believe me the first few times. I could hear her thinking, "Yeah, right. My husband, the same guy with delusions a few months ago, is leaving in twelve hours on some mission? He's full of it."

Aside from all the weird robots, babushkas tugging at roots, and random shooting, my Marines made the best out of all our deployments here. We often arrived in small teams and had the times of our lives. My men worked their asses off while my hair turned more and more gray. I was under the extreme pressures of planning and ensuring the safety and mission accomplishment of our unit. I was more stressed than the top button of a fat man's pants. But these Marines were a breed all their own. They kept me sane with their humor and creativity. They did something new every day that would crack me up.

I went out on a night run. The stars sparkled. The air wasn't too cold and was thin and easy to breathe. Snow crunched. No nose drip for me tonight. The base was quiet. "All the actors must have gone home," I thought as I ran past the abandoned playground. Stress left with each steam puff. My eyes adjusted, and the snow lit up a white path. I thought of my family and what I had put them through. I was never home. I missed birthdays. I missed anniversaries. "I may miss Christmas next week," I muttered to myself.

I was not sorry, but sad. Maybe later in life I could make up for being the dad who was gone all the time. My friend, Captain Collins, had a saying: "You can be a good Marine or a good dad, but you can't be both." I was being a great Marine. Right now, these detachment Marines were my children, and they needed me as much as I needed them. I turned into our tactical compound, and what I saw put a smile on my face that was so big it squeezed out tears of joy. I loved these jokers!

I had been gone for a few hours; during that time frame, they had chosen to decorate our barbed-wire perimeter with Christmas lights. Colorful strings of lights were carefully strung around the perimeter of the camp, transforming it into a merry little Christmas village. The lights made the white snow glow. The camp could probably be seen for miles. I'm sure we were supposed to blend in with the scenery, with our camouflage netting, and stay low-key. But these Marines had made an exception—'tis the season! On top of the entrance was a makeshift Christmas tree with a star constructed out of broken CDs.

Our craziest moments paled in comparison to the strangeness of this base. At least we were all real; we weren't actors. I looked around at the other decorations made out of wires; tools; Meals, Ready-to-Eat; and trash that my Marines had put up, thinking, "What would the general think of our decorations?" The mood in the camp was light and fun that evening. We didn't really give a damn what the general might think. We had to have a little bit of fun. After all, it was Christmas, and we were stuck here until the mission was accomplished.

CHAPTER 14

Watch Out for the Wild Boars

(and Frogs) in Guam

Guam is about half the size of Okinawa, thirty miles long and twelve miles across at its widest part. Our mission was to deploy our detachment to Guam and support an exercise with US Air Force, US Navy, and US Marine Corps fighter jets over the Pacific.

Intercept control is best explained by citing the scene in the film *Top Gun* where Maverick is dogfighting against an enemy jet. We would be the military controllers constantly talking into Maverick's headset, telling him where the bad guys are. A call over the radio would sound something similar to this: "Maverick two-one, single group BRA two seven zero, thirty, seven thousand, hot, hostile."[36] But our calls were few and far between because nothing worked out as planned. Our radar was down, and our radios where dead.

Murphy's Law was strangling us. Here we were with fifty Marines, a $30 million radar, and another $10 million worth of equipment, and nothing worked. It cost about a half million dollars to fly these Marines and all this equipment out here, and we were about as good as the cesspool our site was

---

36 BRA stands for "bearing, range, and altitude." This is the information needed to tell the pilot, call sign "Maverick two-one," where the bad guy is, and the word *hot* refers to the direct aspect of attack the enemy is on. The enemy is coming right at him thirty miles away and is seven thousand feet high. A hostile aircraft is an enemy aircraft.

on. We were a burden on the American taxpayer. We didn't even have potable water for a few days because of a logistical mishap. Until we got water, I had to go out and police the nearby spigot to keep Marines from drinking out of it and getting dysentery. They were like thirsty dogs that kept coming back to sneak a drink of spoiled water. I'd yell at them when they would come near the spigot. "Get away! Go on, shoo!"

Our officers went out and bought some water from the local store before the situation grew desperate. Nothing seemed to come together. Looking back at our performance, I believe that we failed our mission. However, good things did come of Guam. Our time here was good for two reasons: my detachment finally bonded, and the running was spectacular.

We had a lot of downtime to hang out with each other. We played video games, we played cards, we drank ourselves silly, and we even conducted a play. I remember partaking in each of these activities, but the most rewarding was running. Two words describe running in Guam: frogs everywhere.

The frog population in South Guam was exponential, and I am convinced that a link was missing from the food chain. We probably killed one hundred frogs each time we drove our rental car. I cringed each time I heard their bodies flip-flopping inside the wheelbase. FUMP-FA-FUMP-CLANG was the sound frog bodies made when we ran them over.

The first day we got there, I went on a little run with a couple of lieutenants at sunrise. Before we left for our run, one of the junior Marines from Guam warned us about the dangerous boars that ran rampant around the island. "Those tusks are sharp. They can eff you up, sir," he said. "They'll charge you with their tusks and gore you to death." That was enough to make me paranoid.

I had been the detachment commander for about six months now, and it felt good that I had finally established some loyalty among my junior officers. The good-old-boys club had faded, and my detachment was clean and running like a well-oiled machine. I heard a few grunts fifty feet ahead, and then a furry animal dashed across our path.

We freaked out and sprinted back to our site. "Thank God we were spared and okay!" I thought. We made sure to let all the Marines on our site know about these fierce, wild hogs. I stood on the back of one of our seven-ton trucks and looked every Marine in the eye during our emergency-safety huddle. "Don't leave this site alone. Take a buddy everywhere you go. Marines, we don't know how many of these monsters roam this area. We were just chased away by giant boar. This is *real*, people."

A few days later, we were brave enough to drive our three-ton van down that road to investigate where the monsters hid. The road dead-ended in the parking lot of a small theme park called Talofofo Falls Park. Then, we saw dozens of these monsters. A young boy was petting one and feeding it a treat. Dozens hid from the sun in the shaded crawl spaces underneath the cottages. The five-hundred-pound wooly mammoths were, in actuality, fifty-pound house-pet pigs—nice little buggers, to boot. They were the landowner's, and maybe a few belonged to this child. We all vowed to never tell a soul.

Our detachment camped out in an abandoned facility with ten office spaces, which was a pretty good deal when our alternative was a tent. Tents aren't bad, but they get to be a pain when you need to use the bathroom. You have to walk out in sandals through the mud and sometimes rain. I'll take indoors anytime. The building also provided us space for a mess hall. The roof-top had a deck that became a spot for the senior-ranking gentlemen to gather around and drink some beers and smoke stogies. We would make fun of people and tell sea stories under the Pacific stars. We were far from home, but this wasn't a combat mission, so we could relax and dare to have a good time.

Our operation tents were set up over the drain field for the septic tank. After a few weeks, the tanks overflowed into the mud under our tents, and then we were literally working on a pile of shit. When the commanding general came to visit us, he was extremely interested in what his Marines were doing. He wanted to see them in action, so I offered to take him out to our tents. But when he noticed the slushy mud, he decided to spare his nice brown shoes from the muddy crap.

Guam was a beautiful place, aside from our shitty compound and the dead frogs littering the streets. The roads from our site led me up mountaintops with panoramic views of the vast green mountains. Some afternoons, I'd see little sun showers scattered miles away. I would leave our compound and run down a quarter-mile, narrow drive that led out to a larger highway.

Cows liked to congregate in the middle of the intersections. I never thought cows were dangerous, but I never ran through a herd before. I'd never even come close to one. I meandered through the dozen cows. A couple stepped back; whereas, others in the group wouldn't budge. They just chewed their grass and mooed at me. They were stubborn. Would they charge people if they felt threatened? Was I supposed to keep a certain distance? Why did no one in my life ever mention how safe or dangerous a cow is? The cows turned out to be as "dangerous" as the so-called wild boars.

The most interesting animal I ran past was a horse that was tied up in the middle of a grassy field. He looked at me and held his stare for a few counts. I felt as if I knew what he was thinking by his look. He thought how he would give his life to be like me for one day and go on a little run anywhere and explore our big world. He could go wherever he wanted and follow the scents he desired. He could feel the wind tickle his thick, black mane like a breeze of freedom. He snorted and then kept eating his rubbish. I felt for this animal and made a promise to him that if this book ever made me wealthy, I would go back and buy him. I would take him to someplace where horses can run free, and then I would let him go. I could picture him gallivanting in a celebration circle, stopping to raise his front hooves in the air and nicker at me—a horse sound for "Thanks, friend"—and then turning away to charge off across the verdant prairie.

I approached a rural town that didn't have many homes or much traffic. I wasn't sure if the neighborhoods were ghetto. I never checked out the crime rates in Guam. I would later find out that Chamorros—Guam natives—are very friendly and patriotic. An old Cutlass convertible coasted up to me packed full of teenagers spilling out on all sides. Rap base was thumping and rattling the trunk. They looked like thugs, so I braced for some type of teenage prank, comment, or act of aggression. What they did next gave me the chills and would cement my perception of Chamorros forever.

These kids with earrings and tattoos held out their hands as if I were a celebrity. I slapped hands with each one. Then they cheered and clapped as I ran by. I looked down and noticed that I was wearing my Marine Corps shirt. I found out later that the locals love US service members. I assumed that the 944 US Marines who fought and died in World War II to free Guam from

Japanese occupation still garnered respect for all Marines. Guam had since become an American territory, and these were great Americans. I even got a 10 percent military discount at every store I went to on the island. This type of treatment was sparse in mainland America.

My reward for running up this one particular mountain was a panoramic view of rolling, dark-green hills with the ocean in the background. I had worked the past hour to pump my way up, and now it was time to relax on the way down. I freed up my hips and coasted, tightly hugging the side of the road as traffic buzzed by within inches. I was fixated on each car as they came. When they would see me, they would usually make a slight turn toward the center of the road. If I didn't see this adjustment, I'd get ready to jump out of the way. If they came toward me, I would have about one second to move.

After about two hours of running, I passed a house where the people were having a barbecue. They were using wood planks to cook their meat on, and the smell was spectacular. I pondered how the meat was probably fresh, maybe from one of those stubborn cows. I'm sure they had some good local Chamorro sauce to dress up the meat. I was starving. The smell of food during a long run awakens a primitive gene inside me. I become energized and start to salivate, feeling as if I could hunt down some wild game.

The sun began to set behind the large mountain ridge to the west. For a few moments, a bright, violet ray shined between two mountains. The sides of the mountain cleavage were painted with amber and purple lights. This miraculous effect probably happens for only a few minutes during a few days of the year when the sun shines from a precise angle. I felt honored to have seen Guam's secret sunset. Only a run would deliver me such a prize.

I returned to our compound to discover that our equipment was finally operational after a week of trying. The Marines in my unit would never quit until things worked. They were professional, and I was proud to be their detachment commander. I could feel their confidence in me. Once you win the trust of a Marine, it lasts forever. We ended up having a rough time performing our mission, but we bonded as a unit, and this would lead us to victories on our future real-world missions.

CHAPTER 15

Running on the Blood Under China Beach,

Vietnam: My Dad Deserves the Medal of Honor

My dad leaned back in his recliner with his feet kicked up, relaxing for the first time since he started working construction at 5:00 a.m. The voice of ABC's *World News Tonight* anchor, Peter Jennings, was in the background. I tugged at my dad's thick, dirty boot. I was a young boy at the time, and I enjoyed taking off his shoes each night and hearing about his day. I pulled at the second boot and then peeled off his wet socks to reveal some gnarly feet. His toes were crooked, and his foot skin was as tight as a drum and as thin as a plastic bag. His thirty-five-year-old feet looked worn out, like an old man's shoe.

As he chomped on my mom's homemade oatmeal cookies, he noticed me studying his feet. "Don't mess with my feet, and don't ever mess with your feet. Just don't mess with any feet," he said in a warning shout.

"What's wrong with your feet, Dad?" I asked. He told me they were beat up from the Vietnam War, and then he told me the story.

"Our worst enemy was our feet. You had to take care of them to survive. They were always wet from the rain, the rivers, and the sweat. All the moisture would stay in our boots and finally rot our feet—jungle rot, you know?"

I didn't know. I was too young.

He continued. "Always waterlogged and pruned over, like your fingers after swimming for a while. Then they'd start to fall apart. There was always a temptation to pop a blister, scratch some bite from God knows where, or yank off a piece of dangling skin. One of the Marines next to me couldn't stop picking. One day, he ripped off a scab and accidentally a sheet of skin on the bottom of his foot with it. It didn't take long until it got green and full of pus. Finally, we had to carry him. Shortly after that, he was medically evacuated from the whole country to face a life-threatening infection. Still to this day, I'm not sure if his foot made it or if he even survived."

This Vietnam vignette from my dad would be the start of many to follow. All had lessons about survival and making good, simple decisions. I never forgot a single one of them, and I'd use them as a reference tool later on in my Marine Corps career.

In 2013, my dad and I decided to return to his old battlefields in Da Nang, Vietnam, where he fought for his life as an infantry Marine forty-four years earlier (1968 to 1969). This was an opportunity to finally see these places that had existed in my imagination since I was five years old, when I first started taking off his boots. I also wanted to feel the vibe and catch the spirit of this hallowed ground. It was a special place because this is where my fate survived. If he had died, my chances of life would have died with him. I believed that I had a spiritual connection to this place, so I planned a couple of running routes through these mystic locales.

Our resort was built on China Beach, next to Marble Mountain—two famous combat areas. During the war, Marines referred to this area as "Indian Town," comparing it to the anarchistic, chaotic, 1800s, Native American Wild West. In this place, my dad survived mines, enemy fire, naval gunfire, rocket attacks, and ambushes.

The sand underneath the resort had absorbed the blood of many Americans and Vietnamese, and the sea had washed most of it away. Mankind may have come and gone in the past fifty years, but these trees of Indian Town have remained, and they've seen it all. I wondered what they'd tell me if they could talk.

As fate would have it, my foot got infected around the time we went to Vietnam. On our first morning at the resort in Da Nang, throbbing pain from my foot was intense enough to wake me up at 5:00 a.m. It felt as if someone had dropped a bowling ball on my foot the night before. I couldn't fathom having to fight as a Marine with this pain, much less hike miles on the sand and then through hills and mountains.

I had a major problem on my hands—well, on my feet. It had begun a few weeks earlier when a tiny blister showed up on the bottom-center of my foot arch. I had been on a running streak where I would run at least one mile per day and was now at 180 days, so I couldn't let this bring me down. I decided to keep running, even if I had a stump for a foot. It got worse. As much as I'd like to blame my daily runs for the sore's growth, it was my own stupidity that mutated this thing into a monster. I was Dr. Frankenstein.

I made the mistake of asking people for advice on treating a blister. I find that coworkers, friends, and family members love to play the role of doctor and sports therapist when you tell them about your undiagnosed injury. Other Marines prescribed remedies they had either heard about or tried themselves. They had good intentions and meant no harm, of course; however, nonprofessional medical advice is dangerous. I shopped around and heard all types of creative remedies:

- Go to bed at night with your foot in a sock full of Vaseline.
- Pop the blister with a safety pin and rub salt on it because gymnasts do it.
- Clip the blister open with nail clippers and then squirt Neosporin into it.
- Don't touch it.
- Soak your feet in salt each night.
- Don't run (nonnegotiable).
- Go see a doctor.

I disregarded the most sensible suggestion to go see a qualified practitioner or doctor and went with the clipper and Neosporin-squirting options. Weeks later, days before our Vietnam trip, the blister metamorphosed into a painful, raw ulcer that was devouring my foot.

The pain elevated from throbbing to excruciating, as if a hot coal were stuck to the bottom of my foot. I soaked it in a bath and hoped that water would put out the flame and draw out the pain. I freaked out a bit, focusing on the worst things that could happen. What if I have to go to their emergency room? Would it be okay that an American Marine Corps captain seeks medical attention?

After about an hour, the water did its job and dulled the pain. I decided to clean the gunk out of my foot by running on the beach barefoot. The sand will help scrub the gunk out of my infection, and the salt water will flush it out and stop the infection, and then the pain will go away, right? Nope. The sore was now completely exposed to all types of germs, debris, and bacteria. The worst part is that I never considered how polluted the beach might be. Weeks later, I developed a major strep infection throughout my body. It spread to my elbow, both palms, my knuckles, and the sides of my hands.

I set out for my first run along China Beach. I could barely put pressure on my tender foot. I followed the stone path from the resort down to the beach, one careful step at a time. I had to psych myself up to get through this. I chatted to myself. "Who cares about the pain? This is hallowed ground. People fought and died in this very spot, so I can toughen up enough to endure a boo-boo."

I took off my shoes and gently laid my foot down on the sand, which felt like a pile of shattered glass shards. I wondered how I'd be able to run on it. The brown ocean water churned like a washing machine, and the overcast and drippy weather kept the beach empty. My foot was set on fire when I dipped it into the cold water. The pain was maxed out, and my foot was completely numb. This turned out to be a good thing because I knew it didn't get worse than this. I ran the beach barefoot.

I began with a modified stride that more resembled a skip. Minutes later, my stride normalized, and I placed all my weight on the rotten lesion. I thought it would help the scrubbing action. I began to breathe in the ocean air and listen to the breeze and the crashing waves. The whistling trees must have played the same music during the war. I picked up an eerie vibe and suddenly flashed back in time to my dad's stories. I imagined this place in 1968. I could hear my dad's words in my mind: *On this berm is where some Marines hit an improvised explosive device, and the truck exploded fuel all over the men. Some died, and others were burned alive.* It was a horrible picture.

My adrenaline started pumping as I vividly imagined this story unfolding. My dad had written down many of his stories in a memoir with the working title *Pause.* Here is an excerpt:

We mounted three AmTracs (amphibious tractors)[37] at our battalion a couple of miles south of Da Nang. My radioman and I were on the lead AmTrac, and the entire platoon was split between the other two. I would guess our platoon strength at around forty men. I don't remember our mission, but we were headed north between two of the three Marble Mountains and east a quarter of a mile to the beach and then south along the beach.

The road from Battalion to Da Nang was hard packed and a well-graded dirt road, but we eventually turned off the road onto a sugar-sand road toward the beach. We hit the soft sand, and my vehicle was maybe fifty yards in front of number two and number three, spaced about the same behind. We were about halfway to the beach when the number-two vehicle blew up into an inferno of flames, coming to an immediate stop. As fast as I could turn to see the burning AmTrac, my men were jumping out of the flames to the ground eight feet below, all of them with their clothes on fire. My radioman and I jumped to the ground and ran toward our burning platoon mates, as did the men on the trailing number-three AmTrac. We had to tackle the men running on fire, take them to the ground, and extinguish the burning utilities that they were wearing. We put out the flames using the sand on the ground.

All the skin on their bodies that was exposed to the fire hung from them like what would appear to be long gloves pulled down

---

37 AmTracs are amphibious assault vehicles used by the Marine corps on beach invasions. They're used mainly as troop carriers, and there are various versions.

their arms inside out. The very pink and tender meat under the lost skin was exposed. They were all screaming in excruciating pain. As fast as it happened, we put the victims on trucks there from the AmTrac battalion area, which was just ahead at the end of the road to the beach. We loaded the eighteen or twenty burned Marines, and they were whisked into Da Nang to the Naval Air Station's naval hospital located about three miles north of Marble Mountain.

This was the worst tragedy that I ever witnessed, caused by a triggered land mine that blew through the gasoline bladder tank into the belly of the vehicle. After letting the lead tank pass, the enemy detonated the device under the AmTrac with the most men aboard. I can't recall the rest of that day!

In my imagination, helicopters flew from the ocean and buzzed over the chaos. Several smokestacks belched black smoke in the background. A stream of red smoke slowly reached for the sky—possibly a signal marking where the helicopter should land to pick up casualties. Gunshots popped from all directions. Explosions jarred the earth loose. Sleek jets scorched overhead, hugging the atmosphere just feet above the treetops. They suddenly flew straight up and pooped out several whistling bombs. Moments later, a loud smack could be heard and then an explosion. Faint screams and yelling could be heard from only yards away, just beyond the beach berm. People were killing people. Blood, guts, screaming, confusion, and fear created hell's arena. The crashing waves would drown out most of the noises.

It felt surreal to think that, today, the ocean makes the same crashing sounds as when Dad fought there so many years ago in that hell. The chaotic sounds of war would fade away in time, but nature's sounds haven't changed for millions of years.

Waves pushed clear water to the shore. Some of that water rolled back to the ocean, and some of it was sucked into the sand, making little pinholes in the sand from the air and suction.

I pictured what this might have looked like in 1969. The water was highly concentrated with the red blood of fighting men, much like the thick, black slick of an oil spill. Red waves gently crashed to the shore, but in this moment, they carried the blood of the dead. The sand, making those same pinholes, absorbed some of the bloody water.

During my run, there was no evidence of those hellish days. The earth had somehow, in all its wisdom, gobbled up all the bloodshed. All that remained were the ghostly memories of those who still survive today—men such as my dad.

Off in the distance, a fully clothed man—boots, hat, and all—walked up from out of the ocean and to the beach. Water poured off his shirt and baggy jeans. He looked weathered and thirsty. I assumed that he was homeless and this was his bath time.

On the beach was a fleet of circular wicker boats. My dad had told me about these, but I never actually believed they existed. He used to joke about the fact that they were circular and couldn't possibly be steered in a single direction. He told about these boats to highlight the contrast between Vietnam's civilization and America's. In other words, what they did made no sense to us. To them, it worked. He also joked about how they would piss at the top of the river and clean their clothes downstream. I'm pretty sure that story wasn't real.

I leaped over a shard of glass and looked around for more and saw garbage *everywhere*. The berm opened up to a dry riverbed filled with garbage—a dump. Nothing was organized. All types of crap were just scattered around as if a cargo jet full of garbage had crashed there and scattered tires; trash bags; shopping carts; wood; a bathtub; millions of multicolored, differently shaped, plastic containers; rusted car frames; mattresses; a boat motor; the frame of a child's pink bicycle; and a potpourri of other trash. Garbage bags covered the ground like infested mushrooms. A few garbage fires blew hazy, black silt into the air. The burning plastic smell was the same as those trash fires in Afghanistan.

I was about a half mile from my starting point. I saw my father in the distance puffing on a cigar. I wondered what he saw on this beach. Did certain people come to mind? Was he thinking about the time he got a migraine and was ordered to go to the hospital? The corpsman believed my dad had malaria because he had lost forty pounds in a matter of weeks and was having horrible migraines. It turned out that he was suffering from malnutrition because he wasn't eating. He hated the sea rations because, according to him, they tasted like a burnt rubber hose.

I finally made it back. I had run about four miles. I was too busy thinking about this place and the energy from all its past to even think about my foot. Dad looked calm and peaceful. I think the whole ordeal was all too surreal for him to process. During our entire trip, he didn't show any negative emotional reactions. I asked him if this was difficult for him, and he said quite the opposite. He said it was a great thing to see that life had continued on here. He said it was like coming full circle. The last time he had set foot on this ground, it was to kill the enemy and to protect other Marines. This time, he was here to make peace with his past and learn a thing or two about the fresh, young Vietnamese culture unadulterated by war.

During one of our battle-site tours on a spot called Hill 455, we crossed paths with a man who had fought for the other side, the Viet Cong. My dad and he had very interesting conversations. My dad asked him where they had hidden and what type of weapons they had taken from the Americans. It was so strange to see both of these warriors put their past differences aside and show the utmost respect for each other. They even hugged!

While we were there, I finally got my dad to try Vietnamese food. He had always talked about how horrible their food smelled. He claimed that he had never eaten any of it because of the sour, burnt stench. On this trip, he set aside his previous opinions and approached everything with an open mind.

The next day, my foot was feeling a bit better, so I set out for Marble Mountain. The monster lesion would come back later on when I returned to Okinawa, but it was fine for now, so I took off. Minutes later, I was running through the alleys of the shopping district on the south side of Marble Mountain. The roads were gravel, and the shops were mostly stores that sold a variety of marble figurines. The prices were fairly crazy. You could buy a tiny marble statue of a lion for $5 or a life-sized one for $10,000—free shipping.

This was a strategic location during the war when the US military had an airfield here. My dad had spent most of his time patrolling this area around the Da Nang air base, between the beach and Marble Mountain, less than a mile. This is where he'd performed his most heroic action, the kind of heroism that has won some service members the Medal of Honor. He had been robbed of a great medal, however, and given a good medal. The citation explains his story best:

> Participating in two major combat operations and in over two hundred combat patrols, he boldly exploited each contact with the enemy to the maximum extent as he skillfully maneuvered his men to inflict numerous casualties upon hostile forces. On 21 March 1969, the Second Platoon of Company G was manning a tower, when two tanks patrolling the road below came under a heavy volume of enemy small arms and rocket-propelled grenade fire. Rapidly assessing the seriousness of the situation, Corporal Bolender unhesitatingly organized his Marines into a repelling force to provide protective cover for the tanks. With complete disregard for his own personal safety, he then raced across the fire-swept terrain to the lead tank, which had been immobilized by hostile grenade fire, and pulled the seriously wounded driver to safety. Ignoring the hostile rounds impacting near him, he secured a landing zone and, requesting helicopters, ably directed the medical evacuation of the casualty. As a result of his diligent and resourceful efforts, the operational effectiveness of his unit was greatly enhanced...

I've tried to upgrade his award with headquarters of the Marine Corps, but I was told it is impossible. My dad had done this on his twenty-first birthday. Think about what you did on your twenty-first birthday.

Over the years, my dad told me numerous other stories, and they all assisted with my own decision-making process as a Marine Corps officer. I've always felt like a better man and a better Marine because of his influence and extraordinary teachings. Good fathers are a dying breed.

Our trip was amazing, and it was one of the most spiritually fulfilling journeys of my lifetime for both of us. My dad is an incredible man and the best warrior I know. I am grateful for his stories, our trip, and our time together.

CHAPTER 16

Stand-up Comedy

"**G**et the fuck off the stage, faggot!" the heckler wailed at me. This was not good. I was at the intersection where complete embarrassment, degradation, and failure meet. I'd just fallen into a well of silent darkness. The room I was in—or, I should say, the stage I was on—was too bright for me to see the fifty or so angry and disappointed faces in the audience. The man cussing at me was angry because I hadn't made him laugh at all for the past six minutes. Others were just disgusted and disappointed at my performance because they felt as if they'd just wasted six minutes of their lives watching me tell bad jokes and burn alive on stage under the silent, bright light.

This was my second stand-up comedy performance, and it was a silent nightmare. They literally turned off the microphone, and I was booed off stage. Most comedians say they bombed several times before they were worth the audience's time. I once heard the line, "A comedian is like a jackass in a well. People keep throwing dirt on him, and then, one day, the dirt gets high enough that he can walk out of the well." I was devastated, but I'd be back.

My family and I were home from Okinawa, back in the United States for good. My priority, besides finding a house, car, and getting cell phones for the family, was to do another stand-up. Okinawa had no opportunities, so I prepared the entire time while there. It was now five years since that quiet, bright night when I was booed off stage. Now, I was ready to go head-to-head with another audience—this time in my own backyard at the Fort Lauderdale Improv.

Just days before the show, I was overwhelmed with an adrenaline-angst cocktail, and it was intoxicating. I couldn't eat, drink, or focus. I was physiologically handicapped and in pain. If I didn't run this out of me, I might start trembling on stage, and once an audience senses the flop sweat, it's over.

These runs I took before my next act were a form of dialysis. My body couldn't process it all, so I had to burn it out, purging the toxins. These runs were more about ridding excess energy than the scenery or reflection, so I chose to run on a treadmill in my parents' garage. They actually used theirs, so boxes weren't completely surrounding it. I had become a jackass-gerbil on a hamster wheel.

While running, I concentrated on visualizing the caustic, nervous energy flow from my head and out through my legs into the ground. After a few days of using the running/dialysis machine, I began to wonder why so many people resort to limiting their running experience by running on a treadmill. This was a garage, not a beach. The only smell was gasoline and cardboard. You have to stay on a narrow, black-belt path. It was lame, but it worked.

I was probably not supposed to do stand-up comedy as an officer, although Rob Riggle, a famous comedian/actor, had played in *The Hangover*, *21 Jump Street*, and *The Daily Show* while he was a Marine officer. I didn't want Marines to know that I was pursuing this in my off time for a couple of reasons. One of them was that I was terrified by the backlash I might receive from the Marine Corps, who are extremely picky and somewhat self-conscious about how Marines are seen in the media. Any deviation of Marine standards that is captured in the media is seen as a major threat to the existence of the Corps. If I were seen as inappropriate, then I'd get fed to the sharks and lose my career. I probably wouldn't be criminally charged, but my reputation would disintegrate immediately.

My other reason for keeping it under wraps was that I wanted Marines to take me seriously. I had to disguise my fledgling-comedy pursuits so that I wasn't found out. I remember carrying around the book *Zen and the Art of Stand-Up Comedy* by Jay Sankey with a piece of duct tape across the front cover title. Some superiors wanted only professional, work-related literature on the job site.

My first stand-up was a two-minute act at the Blue Topaz in Washington, DC. This was a tiny stage—and I mean tiny. It was the size of a sheet of plywood. But hey, there was an audience, and they laughed enough to call it a win. The second was in San Diego at a place I will not disclose, and I went down in flames. It was time for my third at the Fort Lauderdale Improv. I felt pretty good! My best friend, the funniest man I know, helped me write my bits, and this gave me confidence. He would make sure I lasted up there to the end.

I waited with my brother in the audience while the first dozen comedians performed. At least half bombed. I had been so sick from the anticipation over the past couple of days that I felt numb. My ankles ached from how much running I had been doing. I'd done whatever I could not to appear nervous once I got up there. The last thing that I worried about was whom I would follow. If he or she raised the roof, then I was in for a beating from this cold audience. Actually, they are all cold unless you're funny.

I watched the two performers in front of me. An older gentleman told vulgar jokes that weren't funny to anybody except himself. I think the only thing worse than bombing is bombing while talking about penises, farts, and vaginas. One down. The next was a squirrely looking man. He was drunk and crashed in thirty seconds. He wouldn't let it go; he couldn't accept defeat; and he kept rambling. He held the audience hostage. At one point, he unscrewed his prosthetic leg and began drinking a beer with it. Could this be set up any better? What more could I ask for? It was time. DING DING!

I got up there and stood toe-to-toe with over two hundred people. It began with silence. I stood there and let it build up under those bright lights, and then—BAM!—I hit them with the best I had. All the efforts I had put into this—the joke writing, the stressing out, and the double runs—came down to surviving five minutes in the shark tank. I hit them with my best jokes, and they laughed. No hecklers! I missed some jokes, but I pulled it off, and that's all that mattered. I was back on the stage.

CHAPTER 17

One Moves On, Another Is Born

My last tour put me at the Marine Corps Recruit Depot in Parris Island, South Carolina. This is where Marine boot camp takes place. Every recruit east of the Mississippi comes here to take on the challenge of becoming a US Marine. I began my tour here as a series commander in charge of thirteen drill instructors (DIs) and anywhere from 150 to 250 recruits. I was there to protect the recruits and protect the DIs to ensure professionalism was occurring at all times.

At Parris Island, I worked about twelve hours a day, six days a week. The long weeks provided ample running time, and I was able to enjoy some of the most memorable runs here. The base was beautiful, but I'm sure it was hell to all recruits.

This was the Moto Run, a company of 545 of America's newest Marines, with their DIs, jogging in a formation down the main street of the Recruit Depot. Their cadence roared like thunder. The same songs echoed throughout the base this day, as they had here for the past one hundred years.

On seeing their Marine in uniform for the first time, families went berserk. They screamed, rattled, and cried. Girlfriends covered their red, tear-soaked faces and heaved relief into their snot-covered fingers. Proud parents held embarrassing, life-sized posters of their sons in Marine Corps dress uniforms with captions such as, "We love you, PFC Brown!" or "We are so proud, PFC Smith!"

The DIs snickered under their steel masks when they saw all this commotion because there was at least one funny thing each of these young kids would do while stuck at Parris Island. Fathers strained to hold together their stoic faces in an uphill battle to fight back their tears, probably refusing to cry in front of tough Marines. Some old folks cheered on their grandsons with their easy, careful clapping—this wasn't their first ticker-tape parade. This was a joyous event. For some recruits, this would be their defining moment. They had changed, and so would their lives—tremendously.

The new Marines were relieved that this was the last physical training event with their DIs. This was an opportunity for their loved ones to get a glimpse of their chiseled bodies and stiff postures. Families could also stare at the monster DIs who had hammered the Marines into steel.

All types of men and women came here to become a US Marine. Some were dropouts and wanted a second chance. Some hated their lives and wanted a change. Some wanted to get tougher because they had spent most of their lives playing video games. Some wanted to kill the bastards who kill Americans. For those who completed the training, they underwent the most intense transformation of their lives, and the process would define who they were for all eternity. They started out as police officers, criminals, medical doctors, homeless, star athletes, heterosexuals, homosexuals, nerds, geeks, jocks, handsome, pretty, ugly, and so on. But on the Moto Run, they were now all the same. They were US Marines.

The thirteen-week process began the moment they stepped off the bus and onto yellow footprints that are painted on the street in front of the building for recruit receiving and processing. They left their identities on the bus. For the rest of their time at recruit training, they would refrain from saying "I" or "me"; instead, they would refer to themselves in the third person as "this recruit." No matter whom they were before arriving here, now they were all nobodies. They were considered sloppy, untrained animals. Their egos would soon be squashed like rotten grapes.

The first few days were spent going through a systematic screening-and-indoctrination process. They make their last call as civilians to the loved one of their choice. The words they used were scripted on an eight-by-eleven-inch sheet of paper taped on the wall: "Hello, _____. I have made it safely to the Recruit Depot. The next time you hear from me will be in the form of a letter with my address on it." After that phone call, the Recruit Processing Company corralled them through medical, dental, clothing issue, field-gear issue, and uniform issue.

I was able to witness recruits get interrogated over prior drug use during the "moment of truth." They sat at desks in a classroom. A Marine gunnery sergeant stood up front and, in a stern voice, directed them. "Everyone put your heads down." He told a couple of jokes to lighten them up. He explained how honesty and integrity are the foundation of being a Marine and how this is an amnesty period.

"In a moment, I will ask you a line of questions about past drug uses. If any of your answers are yes, then I need you to stand up and quietly step outside of the room. If you lie, we will catch you, and things will get worse. You can technically go to jail if you lie. You will definitely go home. If you tell the truth, then we can try to help you out."

After his fear-filled speech, he turned the lights out, and their heads went down as if they were playing the heads-up-thumbs-up game. He started rattling off questions about cocaine, marijuana, and ecstasy. One recruit walked out and broke the seal for the others. Three more got up. One of the recruits peeked through his folded arms to see if anyone was confessing. The gunnery sergeant slid a desk and then a chair with his foot to make the same noise as someone getting up. This way, the newbies think it's okay to tell. His deception tool worked. A couple more stood up. By the time he was finished, about a third of the recruits fessed up. In the gunnery sergeant's eyes, most who had used had been vetted.

I contemplated about whether this so-called moment of truth left the Marine Corps with honest recruits or just good liars.

Once the new Marines were all bubble wrapped for training, they were marched back to the barracks, called a squad bay. Fifty bunks on each side were perfectly aligned. These bunks with blue-and-white-striped mattresses and pillows—the same used in prisons—have slept tens of thousands of recruits. These beds have probably logged close to one hundred miles after years of being pushed from one side of the room to the other. This would be the new home of these remaining unfortunate souls for seventy training days.

The initial step in making a Marine is to break down the raw material into a moldable product. In the first week, the newbies are broken down into a pile of wet clay. The first morning with their DIs begins at 4:00 a.m. The lights are flipped on. Objects crack against the wall. A stout, 5-foot-11 drill instructor, built like a linebacker, shuffles up and down the center, pointing and flailing his arms as he yells. "Get the fuck up! Get on line! I said get on line." The DIs are not permitted to use profanity, but some rules go unenforced. If the captain, their commander, is not present, they tend to bend the rules slightly.

This is Parris Island, where they make the toughest Marines. If these recruits hang on, they may become Marines and fight for their lives in combat situations at some point. So what damage can a cussword really do? I was never a good example when it came to this area. I cussed like a Sailor because I began my journey as a Sailor.

The DIs never stop moving. They will be on recruits' asses every moment of every day. They burrow into their minds and thrash around like bulls in a china shop. These are the angriest devil dogs in the Corps, and these recruits are vulnerable prey in their crosshairs.

Moments after the DI wakes them up, they stagger to get on line, an imaginary line drawn along the fronts of the fifty bunks on each side. When everyone is on line, the recruits are facing each other, and the center, called the highway, is open for their new masters to run up and down. This is their reset point. While in the squad bay, they will be told to get on line thousands of times. Once on line, they stand at attention with their fists tight against their trouser seams and their eyes fixed straight ahead.

The first time is the same for every group—they don't move fast enough. Actually, this is the case during their entire stay, to some extent. On the twelfth try, they usually get the hang of it, but it's never fast enough. The DIs repeat most of the orders ad nauseam until the recruits complete the task in a timely, correct fashion.

The DIs are demanding. "Put your blouse on! Okay, take it off! Okay, put your blouse on! Okay, take it off. Take it off, I said! Now put it back on!"

The first few days are the most painful for the DIs and the recruits. The latter have to perform the most basic tasks thousands of times. On one of the first training days that I witnessed, I counted twenty-four times that the DIs had recruits put on and then take off their trousers. The DIs have to hold their composure while these confused animals fail over and over to do a task under pressure. I've seen doors with holes punched through the glass.

Ask any DI about pick-up week, and he'll tell you he hates it more than any other portion of the training cycle. The DIs come in every day at 3:30 a.m. and will not leave until 8:30 p.m., after the recruits go to bed. The junior DIs run around and scream, for their job is to be devils who are greatly feared. They are so inhuman that recruits will never see them eat or drink. There is a sea story of junior DIs pretending to sleep while hanging upside down like bats so recruits would begin to think they were vampires. Ever since the recruits arrived at Parris Island, nothing made sense, so they begin to suspend their disbelief. It would not be hard to convince confused and scared recruits that they were in hell, with vampires.

In these first few days, recruit bodies are undisciplined. They turn their heads and gaze at the DIs, which is akin to entering a staring contest with a pit bull. They don't know how to march. They forget to shave. They pee in their pants because they are too terrified to ask to go to the bathroom. They are a mess. The DIs work overtime and get worn out, sometimes to the point of exhaustion or extreme dehydration. The junior DIs have it the worst. But, as Marines are supposed to do, they look out for each other and ensure that every one of them stays strong.

I did my best to ensure the safety of the recruits and the legal protection of the DIs. They were the best Marines I've led, and I had full faith and confidence that they would not mistreat recruits. They may stretch the rules in their favor sometimes, but they never hurt a recruit. They're tough, and sometimes a tough guy may push or get too close. Shit happens. I wasn't there to write citations. Rather, I was there to help them do their jobs while ensuring things stayed professional. Recruits have been known to make false allegations against their devil fathers—especially during the first hell week. Most were absurd, such as, "Drill Instructor Smuckers strangled me and told me to die" or "My DI threatened to kill me."

The officers' job was to investigate these matters, but nine times out of ten they were bullshit allegations. Sometimes, there would be a bit of truth there, but I never did see anything serious. These DIs were there to make Marines, not abuse people. They were some of the best Marines I've seen, and I'd trust my life in their hands any day.

They are humans, like the rest of us, but they have one of the toughest and most stressful jobs. I got to see their human side. They sacrifice time with their families, often having to meet loved ones in the parking lot. One DI went out back every night to see his beautiful new son.

"Hold him, sir," he proudly said as he extended his two-week old son out to me.

Sometimes, I would forget that all these Marines have families. You get used to the professional realm, and you think of them one dimensionally and don't see the layers underneath. In reality, they go home every night to their wives and kids and try to squeeze in some quality time. Again, like Captain Collins used to say, "You can be a good Marine or a good dad, but you can't be both." Single Marines also suffered. Try to date someone when you're available only a few hours a week and inaccessible during most hours of the day. The Marine Corps saps the blood and marrow out of a DI's life. Many have told me that this tour of duty was harder than most combat tours.

One DI screamed at a 6-foot-4, thirty-year-old recruit. "Recruit! What is your second general order! Wha-a-a-a-t are you looking at, you nasty slob? You disgusting piece of shit! Don't look at me. Get out of my sight. I said get *away* from me!"

Three other DIs surrounded the intimidated recruit like sharks, and together they berated the big, frightened newbie. The recruit's eyes bounced around in their sockets like the Cookie Monster's. Tears rolled down his face. This was training day number two, and his civilian soul was leaving his undisciplined body. He was nobody but a recruit.

I have seen hundreds of recruits but have never seen a single one challenge a DI. Their souls belonged to the devil now. They were not allowed to think; they were permitted only to follow instructions. They paid a hefty fine for making a mistake. They would be brought to a sandpit around the corner for a cycle of strenuous exercises.

While in the sandpit, the DIs would pace back and forth like a football coach after a bad penalty. "Stand up. Lie down and do push-ups. Stand up. Lie down and do push-ups. Stand up. Run in place—with high knees. Back down and get your face in the sand. Turn over. Sit up. Do jumping jacks." On and on it would go for days and weeks.

I figured that it takes about four hours for a grown man to surrender his ego to the DIs. In about four days, he will relinquish his entire civilian soul. I thought it was a little sad to watch this process. They changed more in the beginning than during the rest of the training. This was shock treatment, and it worked perfectly. Within twelve weeks, they were stiff robots, highly efficient and deadly. Marines don't forget their DI's name, and their DIs reside in their new Marine consciousness for the rest of their lives, like an angry Jiminy Cricket[38] who would sit on their shoulders and challenge each poor decision. On their last week at "Hotel Parris Island," they go for the motivational Moto Run.

The last Moto Run was extremely difficult for me. This was it for me; my days in the Corps were numbered. I hid my tears in my sweat—not the first time I'd performed this gimmick. The sadness lay in the fact that this would be my last run in a military formation with Marines and my last run as a Marine. I saw these young kids as me sixteen years ago. The end of my career snuck up on me. It came up quicker than I had anticipated. Within three months of being on Parris Island, my medical condition of sleep deprivation reared its ugly head and was back to bite me after my files were rescreened.

I got the call one late afternoon from my doctor. He was frank with me. "Your medical condition is nondeployable, and therefore you are unfit for active duty. We have to put you on a medical review board. Start to think about this phase of your life ending."

---

38 In the Walt Disney Movie *Pinocchio*, the tiny cricket, Jiminy Cricket, wears a top hat and sits on Pinocchio's shoulder to remind him of the consequences of each potential bad decision. He is Pinocchio's conscience.

I knew this meant I could no longer be a Marine. My career was in a terminal phase. The Marine Corps is unlike the other services because all Marines must be fit for duty and be able to deploy. In the US Army, US Air Force, or US Navy, they can shove you behind some desk until you heal or never heal, and they do not have to ever deploy you. If I couldn't deal with sleep deprivation, I couldn't be a Marine officer. I figured this was for the better, for I could potentially be in charge of thousands of Marines. I needed to be bulletproof or else I would be risking somebody's life.

While at Parris Island, I had the best time of my career. I was a jokester rather than a hard-ass—more my true self and something that I had really missed during my service. I had fun, as did most around me. I was at the point in my career when I understood how to be a balanced professional. I could lighten up when things went well and bite down when needed. These guys hardly needed an adjustment. They were sharp. I had to be stern at times, but I couldn't resist telling jokes to put a smile on the faces of hardened, stoic DIs. I was their comic relief. They needed to laugh and relax here and there. When they laughed, they got to take a break from their devil characters. I was the Patch Adams[39] of Parris Island. Here in this strict institution, I forced open a crack and filled it with humor and good times. I believe that my sense of humor put them at ease; it communicated to them that I was there to take care of them and was not a threat. I earned their trust.

I enjoyed running there. The routes are comparable to Okinawa on my *Little Runs Big World* scale. It has an aquatic theme, and this always boosts the running-environment pleasure up a few notches. It's hot, but I have no problems with heat. This place feels like a sauna. The swamps brew thick, humid air, and the clouds blanket the cesspool of heat. Northerners always refer to this climate as the worst-possible misery. The narrow roads bisect a vast estuary made of saltwater marshland and tidal creeks. Beautiful! Tides are so extreme here that the water could easily rise or lower by ten feet, depending

---

39 In the film *Patch Adams*, the main character, Patch, played by Robin Williams, uses comedy as a form of therapy for sick patients.

on the strength of the tides. High tides cover the saw grass, and low tides expose the black, muddy bed that resembles tar.

In the past, recruits have tried to escape the misery of Parris Island by walking or swimming to dry land. They would quickly find out how sticky this muck is. Most would make it a few hundred yards before getting caught. Nevertheless, the scenery is great. Plenty of birds flock and gather along the shores. Parris Island also has the Legends Golf Course, which is one of the most underutilized and beautiful golf courses in the country.

The low country of South Carolina has a grace to it that's hard to describe. It has so many unique attributes, like the serpentine rivers that glow amber in the morning and purple at dusk.

On the runs there, company formations would sing cadences during their hikes. They would sound off facts about the Marine Corps, such as who the commandant was, what year the Marine Corps started, and the max effective range of the M16-A2 rifle. The breeze gently rattles the leaves in the open pine forest as rapid rifle shots pop off miles away at the rifle range. During spring and fall, the roads are mostly shady from the tall pines. Parris Island is a great place to run, but my time was running out.

I knew that this beautiful running terrain would not be accessible to me soon because I had only about eight months left of my Marine life. I had to process this new information. I was instantly undergoing a paradigm shift. Thoughts ran through my mind. This is it? All that training and all these experiences lead to here? What will I do? How will I take care of my family?

While on watch one night, I sneaked out for a much-needed run. I took off on a run into the darkness dressed in all black like a burglar. I whipped down a trail deep inside the forest, knowing I would have this path all to myself. Training events did not occur at night unless it was their culminating event, called the Crucible. Not this night; this place was all mine.

I wanted to be invisible. I wanted to lose myself in the darkness to gather my thoughts before the light of my future appeared on the horizon. I let my mind drift from star to star and from tree to tree. Anything in life was possible now. I was running in an embryo, dark matter, and the space between the chapters of my life—that blank, white space on the page when a chapter ends abruptly, and the writer cannot fill the bottom half of the page. I was sad and excited all at the same time. The overwhelming energy in my body fueled each stride. What would come next? What would I run into? Where would I end up? My run on this night was the same as my blind future. I didn't know where this path would lead.

I spent my last few months as the executive officer of First Battalion at Parris Island, South Carolina. This was the most rewarding time of my career. I was able to ensure that all investigations were handled carefully. I was able to ensure that the DIs' careers would be protected from false allegations. I would also hold the office to ensure that we were professional and safe. After all, parents trusted us, professional Marines, with their sons and daughters.

My time finally ran out, and I became a civilian. One thing that aided my conversion to civilian life was running; I was still on my streak, running every day. This consistency at least in one area seemed to make the adjustment easier.

I was medically retired with benefits. My parents, my wife, and two of my best friends had been my biggest fans during all sixteen years that I was in the service. I wondered who would cheer me on during this next phase. Upon reflection, I realized that we don't always know exactly what the future holds. If you have loving, supportive people there for you, the transitions of life can be more tolerable. I was lucky to have a loving wife, kids, and parents who would be there for me unconditionally.

I also had my running as a sanctuary. As the years have rolled by, I've realized that the reason why I run is not that I am crazy; rather, I run because if I don't, I will lose my sanity. I hope my ankle never breaks.

The US Marine Corps and the US Navy were, in some respects, a long adventure of runs all over the world. Every location I went had some incredible place where I could run. Sometimes, the scenery sucked, but the act of releasing heavy emotions or reenergizing good energy was always divine. I left every run feeling good, as if I were walking out of a church service after my sins had been forgiven. I had run a mile every day for over two years until the day I retired. These little runs had been there for me since day one. I've seen friends come and go; I've been in love relationships that were born and then died. My runs never left me. No matter what chaos went on in my life, my runs have continued as they always have, watching it all, much like the ocean waves breaking on China Beach.

CHAPTER 18

The New Path: Running into the

Hope of Future Darkness

The day I left the Marine Corps, my family and I embarked on a megavacation to Ottawa, the capital of Canada; a bight in the Bahamas; and a quaint beach on the west coast of Florida—oh, and Mickey Mouse. At each place, on each run, I reflected on my career to take inventory of my freshly stocked well of fortitude. These first runs as a civilian were refreshing, with clean air, wildlife, shady paths, trickling brooks, soft terrain, and crashing waves. These *retirement* runs were peaceful and random and provided a perfect place to focus on whom I was.

The first few weeks after leaving the Marine Corps were a major transitional period. As with other major life experiences, I would process this change while running. This time running would see me through a metamorphosis from the identity of a Marine to something else—a civilian, artist, and dad, perhaps?

While in Ottawa, I decided that Canadian air is the cleanest in the world. This place is a giant oxygen tank! Oh, Canada, during your cool and crisp summers, you are a runner's haven. I am lucky enough to have Canadian relatives, and I decided to visit them during my first week after retiring from the Marine Corps. I used to go there as a child, and I remember biking through miles upon miles of green paths. I couldn't wait to return to some of those places that were still stored in my memory like a box of old baseball cards in the attic.

My cousin zoomed in on the Ottawa River Pathway, about five miles west of the enamoring Canadian Parliament. This path spans twenty miles along the Rideau Canal and by the Canadian War Museum and Parliament Hill. My cousin is a consistent cyclist, and he rode to work every day on this route. He is as dedicated and addicted to cycling as I am to running. We planned a time and place to cross paths—not to meet and talk or eat breakfast, but just to cross paths. The sun wouldn't rise for another twenty minutes. But it was summer! I vented when I realized that I was dressed for temperatures in the seventies, the average temperatures over the past week. What I got was a forty-degree wind chill that ripped off the Rideau Canal.

I ran into the wind and flexed my muscles to capture my warm blood. I kept my eyes on the river and zoned out and reflected on where all the time had gone the past sixteen years. I was much like an elderly man looking out on the ocean, wondering how time had elapsed so quickly.

The wet, chilly air reminded me of the cold places the Navy and Marines had taken me, like Great Lakes, Illinois (Navy boot camp), and Quantico, Virginia (Marine Officer Candidates School). In both places, we were always cold and wet, and we marched and sang everywhere we went. That was sixteen years ago, but the memories were as fresh as yesterday's batch. So many memories were unlocked by smells, sounds, weather, and visual symbols during my runs.

Besides the nip in the wind, this run was long and easy. The Parliament looked similar to the British Parliament. It shares a similar clock tower, the kind that Peter Pan or Tinker Bell would love to fly to the top of. A squadron of birds coasted over me and swooped around the tower. Where did they come from? Did they live there, or did they just like the view? They flew wherever they wanted, and they probably knew no home; they simply followed the seasons and the best route that was new each time. Out front is the lush, green lawn[40] of Parliament Hill. This is where my cousin and I finally crossed

---

40 Every Wednesday at noon, hundreds of people come out to Parliament Hill to do a massive yoga session. It's a peaceful, one-hour, midweek break.

paths. Our meeting lasted less than a minute, but he was now part of one of my little-run memories! It felt good to see family, the most precious thing that I had given up during military service.

These early civilian-life runs were all about transitioning from the identity of Captain Bolender to Chris Bolender. For the past eight years, friends and family had introduced me to others as a Marine. "This is my son, Chris. Chris is a captain in the Marines." Marines of lower rank referred to me as "sir," accompanied with a salute.

I used to get all worked up over minor professional infractions. One Christmas Eve, my family and I were entering Kadena Air Base, Okinawa, Japan. My car had an officer sticker on the windshield, and my ID card had my rank. The air-force gate guard had a strict protocol, the same that all military branches follow. If the driver is an officer, the guard is supposed to say, "Good evening, sir," and then salute after he signals him or her to enter the base. The very junior (E-1) guard casually greeted me with zero respect. "Hey, bro," he said. I went from zero to pissed in seconds.

This was not about my ego. It was about how I was once an E-1 and would never have even considered calling an officer "bro." Officers are "sir" or "ma'am" or whatever is their rank and name.[41] He was negatively representing the base and the air force. I began to shout at him about how nasty he was. My tiny car rocked side to side each time I air stabbed him with my pointer finger. My kids covered their ears with their hands and earmuffs as I blasted him. *R-E-S-P-E-C-T!* This type of respect is expected in the military. In my new civilian life, it would have to be earned—there's no protocol in the real world.

Marines are told that every time they don't correct a deficiency, they have just set a new standard. Marines take this kind of thing seriously. Any Marine would judge and correct another Marine for walking in public in shorts without a belt. Male Marines are expected to come to work every Monday with a fresh fade haircut. A Marine will shave every day of his Marine life. Female Marines with long hair are required to pull it back so tight that

---

41 Junior service members are also expected to give the appropriate curtsey to all those ranked above them.

many develop a receding hairline within a year or two. They use a ton of hairspray to keep their hair under control at all times in order to adhere to Marine regulations. On a daily basis, they use as much hairspray as men use shaving cream. Those angry drill instructors who live in their conscious will forever remind them of these standards. I had to slacken up a bit and shift my paradigm. No more "sir," no more salutes. In a way, I had to get over my Marine self. I would have to flush these expectations out of my system.

The Bahamas is a great place to forget it all. In his airplane, my father flew my mother, my wife, and me to Cat Island in the Bahamas. The smooth air is clear enough to see from Florida to Bimini, about sixty miles. From seven thousand feet in the air, the ocean is cool spearmint. All the green islands are surrounded by white sand and invisibly clear water. My dad was doing the usual, showing me all the neat instruments in his cockpit. We landed on a little dirt strip. Great landing! Aren't they all?

After driving for a mile, we arrived at the exotic resort of Fernandez Bay Village. The highlight was paddleboarding through shallow, bright, white-sand saltwater creeks. The water is as invisible as I had seen from the sky. You can see the sea turtles, sharks, and other aquatic life so clearly that when they swim under you, they appear to be suspended in air. The mangroves grow above the high-water mark, standing about five feet tall and looking like stilt houses at low tide.

The sky is clear, and I was in a place that surpassed my notion of para-dise—total peace. I was at peace. I was just another fish in the sea. I went from a somebody to a nobody, and it felt great. We'd return to have drinks at the tiki bar with a view found only on computer desktops. An Australian played the Men at Work song "Down Under" on his guitar, and I cheered him on with a gentleman's cocktail.

This was the first time I felt relaxed in over eight years. I went on a run each afternoon, and my thoughts were silent. I ran by one house that had a milk crate for a basketball hoop. Children ran inside, and their parents came back out, holding them close as they studied me. I was just some weird guy crazy enough to run in the summer's heat. This weird guy was just another American civilian—tourist.

Sanibel, Florida, is a common vacation spot for my family. We've made time every summer to rent the same cottage on the beach.[42] It has a similar feeling to the Bahamas; it's quiet and relaxing. The white sands and breezy trees force you to disconnect from the loud world. I fished for snook[43] and netted bait. To the other tourists nearby, whose fishing poles never bent, I was a Florida boy who knew the secret to catching fish (it's local bait).

My runs were always a bit scary because several years back, an alligator attacked a local lady in her garden. The monster dragged her into the water, and neighbors interrupted the gator's attempt to capture lunch. They formed a human chain to pull her free from the bone-snapping jaws. They eventually freed her, but she died later of infection. Along the edge of the brush, I kept my feet light and remained vigilant, bracing for something to jump out. I ran by tourists—who saw me as another person jogging, not a Marine. This felt great.

The transitional retirement/civilian runs helped me to a place, and they also made a few tears—not the first time I've run-cried. Tears came from thinking about the men I've served with. I thought of their sea stories on the aircraft carrier; the drill instructors who bled to make Marines; and, above all, those smart asses who made life great by building a Starbucks in Afghanistan and stringing Christmas lights on the barbed wire around our perimeter to light up our hidden site. The prestige that comes with being a Marine and the power and respect as an officer all had to be turned in when I left, the same way I turned in my rifle and combat gear. Good-bye, Captain Bolender. It was time to reinvent. It was time to run away and never come back. What would I see next on my new random run? My new life?

Running was my enemy when sports coaches and military training used it as a tool of torture. Then, one day, I had nothing else to do in the middle of the ocean.

---

42 My dearest mother-in-law actually rents it and insists on paying for it each year.

43 Snook are saltwater fish found close to shore and inland in brackish water. They are a favored game fish and cuisine among South Floridians.

Running became my salvation and eventually my best friend. Over the years in the military when I was a nomad, leaving every three years, running went with me to each place. Unbeknownst to me, until after my military career, it gave me the hope and motivation necessary to grow spiritually and professionally.

On Mount Trashmore, running got me off that "prison ship," gave me hope and motivation, and then showed me that persistence could help me become a college football player or whatever I wanted to be. During the fourth-coldest winter in Quantico, Virginia, during Officer Candidates School, running was my blanket in the freezing cold and a time warp. I ran and sang the same traditional Marine Corps cadences my family's legacy has sung since the 1920s. Running helped keep me sane after the effects of incredible sleep deprivation. It connected me with the timeless spirit in Vietnam, where my fate was born and my fate survived. Running every day continues to introduce me to new things and old memories.

My military career is over, but the lessons that I've learned over the years will stay with me for life. Marines have a saying: "Once a Marine, always a Marine." This has all been one hell of a *run* all over this great world. What I've seen was amazing, and what I've experienced was both challenging and rewarding. I've sacrificed my youth for our country, and my kids have given the time with their dad that should be spent with them over to our military. Now it's time to take running with me on the unknown path ahead. What will be my next little run in this big world?

Epilogue

My obsessions in life are consistency and perseverance—both can move mountains. I run every day, but I also drink sixty-four ounces of water every day. I write at least twenty minutes every day, and I do a number of push-ups and sit-ups equal to my age. These all help me stay mentally and physically fit. We are our habits, as the saying goes. This is not a religion or a prescription; this is life. Take the advice you want and take it slow, as Kate Nash says in her song "Navy Taxi," because "it's your life and it's no one else's, sweetheart. Don't let someone put you in a box."

If you want to run and not hate it, then I suggest beginning with short distances. If you are overweight or obese, or if you despise running, pick any point and get to it. Distance and speed don't count for anything; jog to the mailbox and back. Do it *every single day*. One plus one is a streak. Go slow, don't run faster than you can breathe, and take runs that aren't difficult.

Tell your ego to shut up when it's too loud. Remember, your ego will guzzle up the adrenaline batch made by excitement. Let your ego lead you when you need it to. Use your ego to get to the finish line. Drink water. Take off that GPS, at least every now and then. Don't plan routes, and keep it fun and random. Run near water. It's okay to walk. Disregard weather. Find a good pair of shoes at any cost. (I've thrown out piles of brand-new shoes.) Don't go broke on accessories. (I'll change my rhetoric once I'm sponsored.) Run at all times of the day, for being random is fun. Listen to music. Run for you, not for *likes* and shallow recognition on social media. Do what makes you better *every day*. My daily streak stats are as follows:

Failed streaks

- Run one mile per day: January 1, 2013, to April 9, 2013. 98 days!
- Dieting—a constant win/lose battle).

Current streaks:

- Run one mile a day: began May 13, 2013 (still active).
- Run two miles a day: began January 1, 2014 (still active).

Setbacks

I have my own philosophy, but I do not hold myself on a higher plane than anyone else. I have nothing new to say. Setbacks are usually opportunities in camouflage. I'm not sure that a failure is meant to be, as the cliché goes. I believe that you can make it meant to be. The *meant to be* is really *what you've made of it*.

I've had a tremendous number of setbacks. I was hurt several times in high school football. I couldn't get into college, so I joined the Navy to avoid becoming a complete loser. I made the Florida Atlantic University football team, but the NCAA deemed me ineligible because they did not recognize my SAT scores that I took through a military education program. I appealed this decision and won, but this happened after the first season had ended. I never returned. Instead, I began a film club, which was the university's first. We made films for four years and had the time of our lives. Football could never give me the satisfaction that making a film did. Filmmaking taught me that I could actually project my imagination onto the screen. The director's vision is the film.

I eventually made this link to life. With the right set, actors, crew, and script, you can create anything. I went to graduate school but didn't finish because my professor and I had a falling-out. I have a bachelor's degree with thirty-nine graduate credits but no master's degree (which requires thirty-six credits) at Florida Atlantic. I cofounded a company that wasn't paying the bills, so I leaped out headfirst into the most rigid institution in the world, the US Marine Corps. I would pay millions for the experience gained. Yet leaving the company that two partners and I had started devastated my friends. We had started our dream together, and I bailed on them. For years, I felt horrible about this decision, but it opened my eyes to how precious a friendship is. Today, I feel closer to them than ever before because they stuck with me after I was a bad friend. I will be forever loyal to them.

The pressure as a Marine officer forced me to become a runner. The time away from my family taught me to appreciate time with loved ones. My early, involuntary, medical retirement was bittersweet. On one hand, I could pursue my dream as an artist seven years earlier than planned. On the other hand, I gave up the proud title of US Marine Officer. I would never again lead the Marines I loved.

The Department of Veterans Affairs ensured that I would be able to recover from my sudden loss of employment by funding me to attend Savannah College of Arts and Design. I was accepted into the writing MFA program. Our society takes care of veterans like no other country does—it's not perfect, but at least we care, and at least we try. All my mistakes are the dents in life that give me character and personality. We're all dealt shitty poker hands, but we can always draw more cards.

Many people dare to begin a new running routine with some fad-diet program. This usually starts with a New Year's resolution and fizzles out by Groundhog Day. Why is this? How come so many give up? Does running suck that bad? Or do we suck at choosing where and how we run?

Why not choose a sandy route along the beach with crashing waves, cawing birds, and fresh sunlight? You can cruise on a path blanketed with leaves under a shady canopy of trees. Why do we torture ourselves by trying to run our fastest each time, as if we're outdoing our past self? Have we visited or at least thought of all the other options outside?

The problem is that most "bandwagon runners" make running a task rather than a journey. Making running a task forces us to view running as a chore. Most of us enjoy the satisfaction of completing a run more than we appreciate the run itself.

Why do we buy a conveyer-belt running machine for $2,000 when the earth has millions of miles for free and on a much bigger playing field?

I would bet that the average usage of a treadmill peaks in its first forty-five days, after which it mostly becomes a drying rack for wet clothing. Treadmills are short-lived because they inflict torture. Their poor owners dread the whiny hum of the belt endlessly cycling as they obsessively stare at the bright-red timer counting down their ten-minute prison sentence. Why do we make it suck so badly? How can we look forward to staring at a red clock or items in our garage?

We shove our treadmills inside a garage with its file boxes, lawn equipment, and other random objects we stowed out of our sight. Why would any sane person choose to run in this environment? Is anything gained from these runs besides burning calories at the cost of torture and self-produced angst? Why stress yourself by staring at the bin of tangled Christmas lights that you never got around to untangling to find that one burned-out bulb? Other thoughts run amok: When will I clean this dump? For the love of God, how much longer? I've only burned seventy calories in these five minutes of agony?

Explore, damn it! Open up that garage door and escape from all the stress. Unleash your imagination to our big and beautiful world. Get a whiff of nature and all her scents. Run under the stars and in front of red sunsets. Get out there, and you will be surprised at how invigorating a nice run can be, even if it's twenty feet.

Experiencing these senses can take you back to your past. Sounds of a crackling fire become cozy memories of ghost stories in Uncle Bill's cabin. The sweet smell of paste transports me to my kindergarten class, where I napped on my mat and drooled everywhere. (Gosh, I haven't unlocked that memory since that event happened in 1985.) The crisp smell of evergreen trees is loaded with Christmas memories.

Surfing through old memories allows you to take a break from the present. We constantly process new information while sharpening our senses. Observing nature or life in action breaks up the wasteful thousands of one-dimensional images we are inculcated with every day. We are fed constant, predigested media messages while we starve ourselves of spectacular views of the randomness of Mother Nature.

With each day we live like this, we find it harder to get off the grid, think, and reflect. How often do we get away from texts, e-mails, and social media? Text messages never stop throughout the day. What about your own thoughts?

What are the consequences of not stimulating your senses and neglecting reflection and innovation? How many of your senses did you use today? Have you seen, smelled, tasted, heard, or touched anything for the first time today? Have you thought of new things? Did you smell something outside that took you back to a past moment?

We need to mix things up a bit because our brains, our creativity, and our spirituality depend on it. Running is a ticket out of sensual deprivation. It synthesizes the world with your thoughts, stirs your soul, lets you purge, and increases your awareness of your own emotions. Running helps you escape into a world of wild scents of flowers, views of a glowing crescent moon, and the wind at your face. You reconnect with Mother Nature as she washes your stress away into the ether. She has a crazy way of calming humans down.

We will never stop running because we are designed to run. We've been running since our inception to escape from predators. We run today to escape stress and find happiness. To not run is to not escape. We must be considerate of people who cannot run *physically*; they can partake in other activities that will get them running *mentally*. Now, go for a run, and never stop running. In between runs, visit www.LittleRunsBigWorld.com to check out advice from runners all over the world and chime in with your own.

Acknowledgments

I realized after writing six pages, on my first draft of this acknowledgment section, that this is impossible for me. No matter how close I would get in naming each and every person, I knew that I would miss at least one. It is because of this one person, who is equally as special, that I chose not to include names.

I thank everyone who has carried me up the steep hills of life, *ran* with me through the trails of darkness, and sat beside me to enjoy the beautiful sunsets. Cheers!

About the Author

Chris Bolender is a retired Marine captain. He's been deployed all over the world during his military career. He's directed films, served in the US Navy (before the US Marine Corps), and performed stand-up comedy, and he loves to run and write every day in Fort Lauderdale, Florida, where he lives with his wife and two children. Chris has also published a children's book titled *The Monster Dentist.*

As of November 16, 2017
Chris continues his running streaks that started on May 13th, 2013.

Made in the USA
Monee, IL
12 January 2020